A QUIET
WITNESS

A QUIET WITNESS

WHEN LIVING A STORY IS LOUDER THAN TELLING IT

Kristin Salvevold

A Quiet Witness
Copyright © 2024 by Kristin Salvevold

ISBN (paperback): 978-1-960111-17-3

Published by RODNEY K. PRESS

Cover design: Abby Colwell

For Jensyn Marcella

Our sweetest gift–our sleepy sloth–our quiet witness.

*"I praise you because I am fearfully and wonderfully made;
your works are wonderful. I know that full well."*
Psalm 139:13-14

CONTENTS

INTRODUCTION

As a young girl, I had three big dreams for my life: I wanted to be a mom, I believed I would marry a pastor (not even kidding), and I have always wanted to write a book—someday.

The Lord led me to a pastor, and we got married. He blessed me as a mom eight times over! And I knew—someday—He would give me a story to write.

Over the years, people who have either read something I have written or have known about my dream, have asked me when I was going to write my book. I have always answered, "Someday—God hasn't given me my story yet." Maybe that sounds cliché, but it is the truth. Sometimes I felt the nudge and wondered if God was giving me something, but the timing was never quite right.

THIS IS IT. THIS IS THE STORY I AM SUPPOSED TO SHARE.

Even at the beginning of Jensyn's journey, I was not convinced this was the story God had for me to tell. As time went on and I began to see the connections God was making through her life and in the lives of others, it was then that I knew: This is it. This is the story I am supposed to share, and I could not wait to write it—someday.

Casey Van Winkle was one of the teens in our first youth group in Aberdeen, South Dakota. He has since moved to Minnesota, but we have stayed connected with his family over the years. He and his parents were at Jensyn's funeral. Just two days after the funeral, he started an online thread with me and his friend, Lindsay Bednar, who has a publishing business. I thanked him for the message and tucked it in the back of my mind. Maybe I would reach out to Lindsay—someday.

Yes, God had given me my story. But He could not possibly want me to write it so soon after losing her, could He? That made no sense to me. I knew I would write her story someday, but not when the loss was so fresh.

I mentioned Casey's message to my husband, whose response was very different from mine. "What would it hurt to call Lindsay? Maybe just check it out," he said. I was in uncharted territory. I can write, edit, and do all those word-nerd things, but the idea of publishing a book was daunting, so I agreed to set up an appointment with her—maybe—someday.

However, over the next few days, God worked on me. As much as I had wanted to write a book my entire life, I was petrified to actually pull the trigger. The days after Jensyn's death were beyond difficult, and I could not imagine reliving them through writing, but I started to realize that maybe her story would be best written while the details were fresh in my mind. Was my someday suddenly here?

I was reluctant to tell people I had begun to write my book. I thought maybe I would wait a year or two, but my very wise Uncle Leighton said, "The farther you get away from the raw pieces of the story, the less genuine it will feel." The more I thought about it, the more I knew he was right—if I waited too long, the perspective would change, and the message that God can be trusted and that all life is valuable might get lost or watered down. This *was* my someday. So, I ripped off the band-aid and began to write. And I have never enjoyed doing anything more in my life.

I met with Lindsay, and I agreed to write Jensyn's story. I cried the day I signed the contract, and I cried before and during my first publisher meeting. Part of me knew this would be one of the hardest things I have ever done, but it was also my childhood dream come true. My emotions were all over the place. I have never felt so unsure and inadequate yet so insanely excited at the same time. It was a bizarre feeling, but my family was 100% behind me, so I decided to go for it. I could hardly believe my someday was here!

It was excruciating at times—I shed so many tears as I relived the hard days and the good days alike—yet sharing her story is another part of the journey that is difficult to explain. Being able to write these words has been more than realizing a dream. It has been and will continue to be a connection to Jensyn that I will always have. It is an expression and an extension of the heart of my family, who has encouraged me and supported me throughout the entire process. Ultimately, it has been my greatest honor. Truly, every time I closed my laptop, I was so emotionally moved to have had this opportunity. That God had finally given me my someday.

I have no idea what God will do with this book, but if He chooses to continue using Jensyn's story, I cannot wait to see how the rest of her chapters play out—someday.

A LITTLE BACKSTORY

I was a junior at Northwestern College in St. Paul, Minnesota, when I met Chris. My roommate, Gretchyn, was dating his roommate, Barry, and the boys stopped over at our place to drop something off. I immediately thought Chris was cute and could not wait to ask Gretchyn if he was available. He was.

Gretchyn and Barry began to plot our setup. For whatever reason, Chris said no to their first three attempts, claimed he needed to do homework. On a Friday night? What an excuse.

Jodi and Sue, my other roommates, decided to join Gretchyn's mission to help me figure out my love life. There was a special weekend at our college called Roommate Roulette. The idea was that your roommates would set you up on a date (or two) that you must agree to attend, no matter who they set you up with. My friends must have been eager to find me a man—I had not one date that weekend but three!

Chris was date number two, and although I had a great time with the other two guys, his was by far my favorite date that weekend. Even still, it took a double date with Gretchyn and Barry for him to agree to go out with me. I was thrilled that he finally had a homework-free weekend available! The date consisted of homemade pizza and a movie at Gretchyn's parents' house, offering us a great opportunity to really get to know each other. After just one night, I was smitten. I remember calling my mom to tell her I had met someone. After asking me about the date, she asked me his last name. When I told her Salvevold, she gasped and said, "I hope you don't marry that guy!"

If you ask Chris why he turned me down at first, he will tell you I was out of his league. To that, I say, whatever—cue eye roll. He was the kind of guy I tended to gravitate toward but could never get to like me back— cute, stylish hair, trendy clothes, confident nature—a pretty boy of sorts with a charismatic personality, a boy who intrigued me after our first connection. Although we both cared about our appearances (we both worked at clothing stores and spent more than we made), what we liked to do could not have been more different. I often say that we never would have dated in high school: he was a band geek, I was an athlete; he knew everyone in his graduating class, my class had more than 250 people; he can sing, I make a joyful noise. However we matched where it mattered most: we both love Jesus and family means everything. As a young girl, I always believed I would marry a pastor, so when I learned he was getting a degree in youth ministry, I was all in. It became glaringly obvious that in the non-negotiables we were a perfect fit.

We had been dating for about five months when I went on a Spring Break mission trip with a leadership group from college. Our focus was to enhance a camp called The Oaks for inner-city kids in California. While on this trip, I was able to fully focus on God and spend some time praying about what He desired for my future. Before this, I had been so obsessed with my new relationship with Chris that I wondered if this was causing me to forget about my most important relationship.

Upon my return, Chris and I went for a walk at a park close to the college, and I shared my heart. This led to me breaking up with him. Neither of us saw this coming because it was not my initial plan even after my reflection on the trip. But the more we talked, the more obvious it became for me. Regardless, both of us were heartbroken. God was impressing this on my heart, and I knew I had to obey. But it still felt like genuine loss to me. It was a test of true obedience of my faith. Trusting God to handle my heart was not easy, and giving up control has never been effortless for me. Fortunately, it soon became clear that the lesson was in my readiness to obey, my willingness to give up what had become too important.

Shortly after we broke up, it was apparent that although we could have survived life apart, we were definitely better together. Seeing him sit somewhere else in chapel each day was miserable, I hated eating lunch without him, and our shared locker felt empty without his stuff. This relationship I had taken for granted—the connection that had previously been given the wrong spot in my heart—was finally being put into proper perspective for me.

Chris was patient and gave me my space, but I will never forget the day he visited me while I was working as a teacher's assistant for one of my professors. I was pleasantly surprised to see him standing in the office doorway. "Hey," he said tentatively. "I'm Chris. Will you go out with me . . . again?" Easy, yes. Our fresh start. A renewed perspective. It was exactly what we both needed to continue living out our story—this time with God's blessing.

After getting back together, we were inseparable, and within three months, we were engaged. Chris proposed to me in the campfire room at Faith Haven Camp, a camp his grandfather helped build and where Chris and his family had lived and served since he was a young boy. A year later, upon graduating from college, we were married in my hometown of Aberdeen, South Dakota. Two weeks after our Cancun honeymoon, I began my first full-time English teaching job at Irondale High School in New Brighton, Minnesota, and Chris started his first year at Bethel Seminary in Roseville, where we lived in married housing.

While a student at Bethel, Chris began to get the itch to put his youth ministry degree into practice. We had received a letter from my home church in Aberdeen, which stated they were looking to hire for new ministry opportunities. Chris contacted the senior pastor to inquire about becoming the first-ever youth pastor at First United Methodist Church. He got the job, so we left our beloved Minnesota to move to my hometown in South Dakota. We loved our life together, and even with the transitions that occurred during our first two years of marriage, we were ready for whatever God had for us next.

As most young couples do, we had discussed when we wanted to start a family. It was our belief that married couples should have a few years alone before having kids. Neither of us had big families growing up (he has two siblings and I have one), and we agreed that two or three kids would be the perfect little family. In order to ensure we did not have a baby too soon, I did what all my newly married friends had done and went on the birth control pill. It did exactly what it is marketed to do—it controlled my fertility.

After living in Aberdeen for almost a year and being married for three years, we decided we were ready for a family. I got off the pill, assuming pregnancy would soon follow. It did not. After trying to conceive for almost a year, we consulted a doctor. Dr. Wachs said that one year of trying did not constitute infertility, but he prescribed Clomid anyway. We filled the prescription, but I never took a pill from that bottle. To have taken the medication would have felt like we were "playing God" in a way that would demonstrate a lack of trust in Him. We opted to keep trying without the help of meds to see what God would do.

A few months after our initial meeting with the doctor, we finally got the news we were waiting for. It was May 1998, and I was finally pregnant! Not once did I think anything could go wrong, so we told everybody, even though I was just a few weeks along. To announce the pregnancy to our youth group, we created a relay of baby games for them—eating baby food, drinking out of baby bottles, munching on chocolate chips from a diaper, and so much more—and it was soon obvious that we had big news to tell. Some moms cautioned that we should have waited longer to share our news, but we believed that God would not let anything happen to our baby after all we had gone through to get to that point.

Looking back, I can recall some moments where I began to suspect something was a bit off. However, since it was my first pregnancy, I did not have a reasonable frame of reference. Initially, I was appropriately nauseated and felt all the pains of a changing body. At one of my early appointments, I remember chatting with my nurse and telling her that after feeling sick and uncomfortable for a few weeks, I no longer "felt" pregnant. She replied that each pregnancy was different and did not share my concerns.

A few weeks later, Chris and I were at his family's house for Memorial Day, and I was exhausted, but I still had my suspicions that something was wrong. Toward the end of that weekend, I started spotting. We called the clinic and they assured us that it sometimes happens in the first trimester; a little bit should not be alarming. By the time we got home, however, it had become evident that I was miscarrying my baby. An appointment with our doctor the next day confirmed this reality.

It was roughly three weeks between finding out we were expecting and losing our baby. Devastated. Confused. Afraid we would never be able to conceive again, we were baffled as to why we were going through this challenging journey. It was the first time our marriage had ever taken a hit, and we wondered where God could be. Chris and I were not emotionally or spiritually prepared to deal with the loss. We had questions for our doctor, and they answered that this often happens in women who had been on the pill. I was told that it was possible my body needed a reset of sorts. We had questions for God: Why was having a baby such a struggle for us? We had waited for each other, had waited until we were married. We loved God separately and served Him wholeheartedly as a couple. Why were teenage girls being blessed with a baby they did not even want when this

> NOT ALL MISCARRIED BABIES GET A NAME, BUT WE WANTED TO GIVE ONE TO OURS.

same blessing was being withheld from us? So many questions. I could only speculate on the answers.

Something I learned from my miscarriage is that it is impossible to truly empathize with others unless a person goes through a similar loss. There have been many times in my life when I have been able to commiserate with someone else who has suffered a miscarriage even though the pain and loss affect each woman differently. After I had my first three babies, I remember thinking that if I had just known at the time of my miscarriage that we would eventually have children, the loss would have been easier. Yet, through my pain and my growth, I could see that God needed this struggle to be my reality so that I could clearly see each life as a gift. Being able to have children is not guaranteed, and I believe that if we had gotten pregnant right away and had never gone through that initial loss, it would have been much more difficult for me to grasp the immense value of the lives we have been given. I wonder if I would have taken for granted the ability to have children at all.

Not all miscarried babies get a name, but we wanted to give one to ours. At eight weeks, we did not know our little one's gender, so we thoughtfully chose a name from our list that could be used for either a boy or a girl: Jamie. Making this decision set the stage for our concrete belief that every life is valuable; every baby has a soul. By naming Jamie, we gave this child his or her rightful place in our family from the start. Jamie has always been part of our story. Our first child. Our first loss.

Shortly after my miscarriage, I was at a women's retreat with some friends from church. There was an open prayer time at the end of the weekend, and I knew I had to put aside my pride and share my deepest longing as a result of our loss. The ladies prayed over me and begged God to bless us with a baby. This moment became a significant spiritual marker in my walk with Jesus. Shortly after the group finished praying, a woman I hardly knew but respected for her great faith approached me and asked if I had ever considered allowing God to decide the size of my family, whatever that might mean. Nobody had ever asked me that question, and the thought of giving up control was daunting. She then asked if she could give me a book entitled *A Full Quiver* by Rick and Jan Hess. Since books have always been my love language, I agreed to read it, and through it, God began to shape my view of how our family would be defined.

I devoured the book and shared it with Chris. The conviction to allow God to decide how many children we would have was realized, and we have never questioned it or looked back. At that point, we were not foolish enough to believe we would immediately be blessed with another pregnancy, but I know this was where God needed us to be—open, expectant, and content with whatever He chose to do. It felt overwhelming, but we also had great peace.

By August 1998, God did choose to bless us with a baby, and Max Christopher was born in April 1999! First-time parenting was not easy, but at the same time, it was everything we had hoped it would be. Because of what we had gone through—the waiting, the uncertainty, and ultimately the loss—our gratefulness for this life that had been given to us meant everything. All of these pieces began to form our journey as a family, a family who had given control to God and who would do all that we could to leave it there.

Although we had begun to see the eternal value of life, there would come a time in our journey when we would be tested. God knew there would be more difficulties where this value would not only be challenged but would also be questioned by those watching our story unfold.

ADDING CHARACTERS

After Max was born in April 1999, we maintained our commitment to be open to whatever God had for us regarding our family size. We loved being parents to our sweet little boy. Chris continued his job as a youth pastor, and I became a full-time stay-at-home mom who coached a little volleyball on the side. Of course, we took Max everywhere possible as I still wanted to be involved in ministry with my husband. The church family and my volleyball girls quickly fell in love with Max, and he became very comfortable around people. His charisma and personality were effervescent, even at a very young age.

In September 2000, we were excited—and a little nervous—to learn I was pregnant again. Regardless of how many miscarriages a woman has, I suspect there's always a nagging "what if?" I was understandably nervous that I might experience another one. This time, we waited until I was through the first trimester to tell people our news, but it was soon obvious that pregnancy number two was sustained. In May 2001, Maci Lee was born. Although I loved having a boy first, and Max truly was my little buddy, I so deeply desired to have a baby girl. Maci was spirited and so much more dramatic than her brother, but differences aside, we recognized her as the amazing gift she is to our family.

Parenting two kids was an adventure, and we loved the challenge! This was what my family had been growing up: mom, dad, one boy, and one girl. It is what I knew. One child of each gender is great—a "complete" family, some would say—but something had changed inside of me, and I found myself hoping that God would bless us with more. Max had just turned two when Maci was born, but things slowed down after Maci. After all we had gone through, I wondered if this was it for us, if God's plan for our family was only two kids. I vividly remember driving by myself on the back roads of South Dakota, crying out to God about this very thing. Through my tears, I felt God impress upon my heart that I would have another baby; it would be a girl, and I was supposed to use the name Amy. Amy was the name of my favorite childhood baby doll, the middle name of the grandma I was closest to, and the name of Chris's sweet cousin, who had passed away when she was four. It was a crystal clear picture, and I remember feeling genuine excitement for what was to come. What a gift it would be to use that precious name!

For more than two years, we enjoyed life as a family of four. In February 2004, we found out that we would add to that number. As if adding another child to the mix was not life-altering enough, we also felt the call to move back to Minnesota to serve

TWO TO THREE WAS THE HARDEST, SO AFTER THAT, WHAT'S ONE MORE?

at a new church, which we did when I was eight months pregnant. In August 2004, Chris began as the youth pastor at Becker Evangelical Free Church in Becker, Minnesota, and in September 2004, Tygen Dean was born.

Life for our family was different and exciting, wild, and exhausting. Max had started kindergarten, I was at home in a new place with a three-year-old daughter and a brand-new baby boy, and Chris was navigating a new job. It is a good thing that Tygen was such an easy baby. Perhaps I had gotten the hang of this mothering thing, but I am more than willing to give God the credit, as He knew the kind of baby we would need then. We often get asked: "Which kid transition was the hardest?" and I always say that going from two kids to three kids was the most difficult. That would have been true even without the chaos of the move and life at the time.

Maci was three when Tygen was born, and that was a nice, doable age gap, but shortly after Tygen turned two, Tate Jeffrey was born in January 2007. Tate was another sweet boy, but he had a few reflux issues that kept us awake and searching for answers. It is never easy to see a baby struggle. Time leveled out his issues, and we soon saw that the transition from three kids to four had not affected us very much.

Three boys and one princess—Maci and I were outnumbered. I often thought about my prayer time with God, where He had shown me a clear picture of another baby girl in our family that I was to name Amy. Was that going to happen? I had been blessed with two boys since that time with the Lord, so surely, this was a reminder to keep trusting Him with our family. So we did, and Brinkley Amy was born in December 2008, just shy of two years behind her brother, Tate. The family was getting bigger, and the babies were coming closer together. But as I always say, "Two to three was the hardest, so after that, what's one more?" Brinkley was a sweet baby, and having another girl was fun!

The thought that Brinkley might be our last baby had crossed my mind since I had finally used the name Amy, but again, not even two years later, Britlyn Ann Marie was born in November 2010. Britlyn was our tiniest baby and remained overly small for the first few months of her life. She was the easiest, most content, most agreeable baby of the bunch, but we soon saw that something did not quite add up with her development. Not only was she not gaining appropriate weight, but she also was not reaching milestones that our other children had met. Doctors were not concerned and continually said that every child develops differently. I might have accepted that response if I had not already been a mama to five other children. We continued meeting her needs at the time, yet we were confident that something seemed more than off with our teeny girl.

In October 2011, when Britlyn was eleven months old, we discovered we were pregnant again. At the same time, we had begun early intervention to meet Britlyn's ever-increasing developmental needs. In April 2012, Britlyn received her diagnosis: a deletion in her tenth chromosome. At the time, we knew nothing of what that meant, but it was an answer of sorts to explain what was affecting her life.

In June 2012, her baby sister Jakely Jami was born. These girls had the closest age gap, and we wondered what God was doing. Britlyn had weekly physical therapy, occupational therapy, and speech therapy appointments, and we still did not understand what Britlyn's future would entail. Yet God chose, in his infinite wisdom, that I would get pregnant even before receiving her diagnosis. If we had known that something was wrong with our child, we might have begun to wonder if it could happen to another child, which might have made us second-guess our unlimited child agreement with the Lord. Another pregnancy before we knew Britlyn's diagnosis left no time to make a decision one way or the other—He decided for us. God knew that Jakely was exactly the baby we would need then, and she has been a blessing to our family ever since.

EDUCATION EDIT

As our family continued to grow, life became a blur at times. Parenting is hard work no matter how many children one has, and we did our best to meet all the needs of our kids while simultaneously challenging them in their independence and growth.

Shortly after Max started kindergarten in Becker, I had Tygen. Life for Max was anything but normal. We had just moved to a new place, he had left a set of his grandparents, his mom had just had a baby, and we expected him to jump into a new school setting and flourish. As it often goes, that did not happen. He hated school—HATED it. He would cry every morning and be miserable even after being there. He had done two years of preschool in South Dakota without any issues. Learning was easy for him, and he loved going to preschool, so we had to wonder what else was going on. It was not until the second half of the year that he began to tolerate school.

During this transition into kindergarten, we were meeting so many new families at our new church. We started to notice that many of them were homeschooling families. I have a degree in education and had taught in public schools for several years. I chose the field because my mom was a teacher, and her schedule was perfect for working and managing a family. To be honest, homeschooling had never been a thought in my mind! I held the stereotypical notion that only weird families schooled their kids at home. I wanted my kids to go to school where I could get obsessively involved in their classrooms and be *that* mom. And someday, when all my kids were in school, I would use my degree again.

As Max's kindergarten year went on and he continued to struggle, God worked on adjusting some expectations we had for our family, and again, He called us to consider doing something we had never thought of doing before. It soon became abundantly clear that educating our children would become our job and that we would begin homeschooling when Max started first grade.

We brought Max home the following year, although we still sent Maci to preschool twice a week. She needed to learn that other people, besides Mom and Dad, had rules they expected her to follow, and we hoped that it would help me get into a good routine with Max. When Maci was home, we did school with her as well. We agreed that we would take things one year at a time and always do what was best for each kid, doing our best to give them what they needed.

After that first year, I was confident we would remain a homeschooling family for the rest of our kids' school years. I saw the value in being with my kids for the best hours of their day rather than just getting their leftover hours at the end of the day. Being able to teach my children to read or being a witness to their excitement when they figure something out are things that bring me great joy. Ultimately, I can focus more on character over curriculum in their overall development, which has meant everything for their self-esteem and the successful functioning of our family.

Socialization, or the lack thereof, is one of the most-cited concerns from families who question homeschooling. Initially, we worried about this as well. Chris and I loved school, and both of us had gone to public schools, where the majority of emphasis seems to be on peer-to-peer connections. As soon as we decided that we would homeschool, it became our goal to ensure that our kids had plenty of opportunities for socialization. Yet we quickly learned that sibling bonds, connections with other adults, and our individual relationships with our children proved to be a better gauge of genuine, long-lasting socialization. Being involved at church through children's ministry and youth group and participating in public school sports or school musicals was another way our kids made friendships and built connections in the community.

After homeschooling for several years, the teacher in me yearned to get back in the classroom. I have never returned to using my degree in an official setting, but I did link arms with like-minded homeschool moms to begin a co-op in our town. What started with about six families has grown to over fifty families and continues to meet the needs of those in our community to this day. Not only do I get to teach writing, speech, and literature to middle and high school students, but my kids have also been students of other moms who excel at history, science, and the arts. This win-win decision proved to be very valuable in our educational journey.

So what about our initial perception that all homeschooling families are weird? As a teacher and a coach—and with Chris's experience as a youth pastor—we came to a very profound conclusion: kids are only as weird as their parents. Not sure what that says about us, but we have been told that our kids are "pretty normal for being homeschooled." Either way, after graduating three and still working with four, we are forever grateful that God called us to do this, and our kids would wholeheartedly agree.

Homeschooling is a lot of work, and being responsible for my children's educations is all-consuming—yet we kept having babies even amid the crazy. Anytime a new baby joined the mix, it was often difficult to find the balance again in our days. Sometimes, I would work one-on-one with Max so that Maci or Tygen could entertain the younger kids. Often, I would be nursing a baby while teaching, or I would have to wait until naptime to be able to concentrate fully on the older kids. Homeschooling is not always easy, but we have found ways to make it work. The flexibility is definitely a huge perk of homeschooling. Looking back, it is apparent that God used this flexibility to prepare us for what was to come. He knew we would soon need to rely on each other daily to fulfill the mission we were being called to live.

GENETIC TYPO

Parenting seven children seems like a lot to most people, and at times, they would be right. I often get asked how I manage with so many kids, but I think the truth is that it does not matter how many children someone has; parenting is hard work. And it was. It still is. But nothing else in life has been more rewarding.

If parenting typical kids is difficult, adding a special needs kid to the mix definitely increases the crazy. My first five kids were not without their individual idiosyncrasies, but their quirks simply added to their personalities and their unique places in our family. When Britlyn was first born, she was so tiny, so sweet, and so adored. Truly, everybody loved this girl. Even her badly crossed eyes somehow added to her cuteness. Yet, the summer before her first birthday, we were faced with a situation where it became painfully evident that something might be wrong with our little Bitty.

We were at the lake with extended family, and Chris's cousin, Rachael, was there with her son, Elijah, who is one month older than Britlyn. Britlyn was sitting with Grandpa Lowell, and Lowell's brother was holding Elijah. Elijah was looking around, reaching up, and touching things around him. In stark contrast, Britlyn's head was down, her chin on her chest, and her arms stuck to her sides. She was not interacting with her grandpa at all. She was just sitting there. The picture of the two babies sitting by each other is still so vivid in my memory. One child was flourishing and doing all the normal things a nine-month-old would do; the other child, my child, was doing nothing. We could no longer ignore the signs.

WE COULD NOT HAVE IMAGINED ALL OF WHAT WOULD UNFOLD IN THE COMING MONTHS.

After that weekend, we visited her doctor to tell him what we had observed. With the information we provided, along with her ever-increasing crossed eyes, he decided it was best to have someone else weigh in. He referred us to Minnesota's Help Me Grow program, which "connects families to resources that help young children develop, learn, and grow." A referral was also sent to an eye doctor who worked with the InfantSEE program, and that's where we began to get answers on her vision issues. Finally, her pediatrician agreed with our pleas to get some answers, and although we needed answers, we could not have imagined all of what would unfold in the coming months.

Along with her crossed eyes, Britlyn had other issues with her vision. While she was still very young, she had hated to lie on her back for any reason. When lying down, her eyes would roll back, and she would arch her body, obviously in discomfort. She also did not do well outside in bright sunlight, and we could not get any photos of her with her eyes open. Vision was clearly an issue for her. Dr. Gregory was the optometrist we saw in the InfantSEE program, and after so many months of wondering why Britlyn's eyes were so sensitive, her professional guidance was such a gift. Dr. Gregory suggested we have an MRI to ensure that all was healthy in, around, and behind her eyes, so we scheduled one but had to wait a bit before it could actually take place.

Meanwhile, the Birth to Three team of Help Me Grow came to our home to assess Britlyn's development. Britlyn did not roll over until she was seven months old, could not lift her head or reach up with her arms at nine months old, and could barely tripod-sit at ten months old. The therapists who tested Britlyn confirmed that her overall development at ten months was that of a six-month-old.

It was evident she would benefit from the therapies they could provide, so Britlyn received occupational therapy and speech once a week and physical therapy once a month. We were so grateful Britlyn was getting this help, but it did make things much more chaotic for our family. This was our first exposure to allowing people we did not know into our home to provide services we could not provide on our own. Yet, we collectively agreed we would do whatever we had to do to get Britlyn the help she needed.

Britlyn finally had her MRI when she was eleven months old. When we met with her neurologist to get the results, we were told the MRI was normal, but then he shared a list of physical characteristics that were "unique" to Britlyn: deformed features, bulging forehead, eyes too far apart, the bridge of her nose too wide. These findings led to another referral: it was time to see a geneticist. While we waited for this appointment, her neurologist recommended that we increase her therapies because Britlyn was still not saying any words and was not even close to being able to walk. Occupational therapy and speech would stay at one time a week, but physical therapy would change from once a month to twice a week! Because the Birth to Three team could not accommodate this change, we began our adventure into outside therapy and started going to NovaCare in Monticello, Minnesota. At this point, Britlyn went to therapy twice a week and had in-home therapy once a week. Again, we wondered how long we could keep up this pace, but we knew we would do whatever it took to get her the help she needed.

Britlyn's genetics appointment finally happened when she was sixteen months old. They took as much blood as her little body would allow. The appointment was quick, yet it took a full month before we got the call that brought with it a diagnosis. It was a diagnosis that did not really mean much to us at the time but one that would forever mark our daughter as different. It was a diagnosis that gave us more questions than answers. A diagnosis that exposed us to the world of genetic disorders, which felt much like being tossed into the deep end of an enormous pool without the means to swim. We had kept things afloat for as long as we could by ourselves, but it soon became obvious we needed even more help; at the very least, we needed someone to show us how to tread the water surrounding this now-defined twist in our story.

Britlyn's official diagnosis did not feel very official at all. We learned that she has a deletion in her tenth chromosome, but this deletion is not part of a syndrome—it is just a tiny 10q26.2 deletion. We learned that a chromosome is made up of telomeres, and the tenth one has 26.3 telomeres on the q arm. She has an entire chromosome except for the 26.2 and 26.3 telomeres. Amazingly, this tiny deletion on each of her tenth chromosomes is enough to affect so many parts of her physical, emotional, and mental health. The significance of this condition made the verses from Psalm 139:13-14 take on new meaning for us: "For you formed my inward parts; you knitted me together in my mother's womb. I praise you, for I am fearfully and wonderfully made. Wonderful are your works; my soul knows it very well." Our bodies are so intricately made that even a minuscule deletion makes a massive difference.

Because her genetic condition is not associated with a specific disorder, it is listed as rare. We were not supplied with much information about what to expect, so we just embraced the unique child we had been given and vowed to do whatever was needed to provide for her as much success in life as we could. The internet is a vortex at times, and a person can go crazy chasing all of the "what ifs," but connecting with others who have children farther ahead in the journey was both helpful and unsettling. I was able to virtually meet other moms to ask questions that pertained to daily life with a 10q child. Some of the other children were high-achieving and flourishing. Others remained nonverbal and immobile. At this point in Britlyn's journey, we were unsure what her future would hold.

Just two months after we received Britlyn's diagnosis in April 2012, her sister Jakely was born in June. Jakely was a big baby at nine pounds, and Britlyn, at eighteen months, was only sixteen pounds. Because Britlyn still could not walk and because she was so tiny, we carried both girls in car seats wherever we went. This meant outside therapy appointments were difficult for me to do alone. My big kids became my support, and the rotation of attending Brit's weekly appointments with Mom had begun. Max was thirteen, and Maci was eleven at this time. It became our collective goal as a family to serve their sister as we did everything we could to help her navigate her development—all while welcoming a new sibling into the family. Weekly therapy continued at home, but her other therapy moved from NovaCare in Monticello to SPOT (Speech, Physical, Occupational Therapy) Rehabilitation and Home Care in St. Cloud. This meant that her appointments were farther away, and it was a struggle to juggle a newborn and a nonmobile toddler.

In the fall of 2012, Britlyn was still nonverbal. Even though we had taught our kids basic sign language as babies and toddlers, we decided to learn as much sign language as possible as part of our homeschool curriculum since this would be Britlyn's primary form of communication. The kids were excited to learn more signs, and Britlyn quickly learned some of the basics. She even had a sign for each of her siblings that was unique to them. During this time, we also began meeting with other specialists: she saw nephrology for her tiny kidneys, a cardiologist performed a heart echo, and she had repeated hearing tests with her audiologist. Although her kidneys were small, they functioned appropriately; thankfully, the heart echo results were normal, but she continued to fail her hearing tests. Because of these repeated failures, Britlyn was referred to an ENT at Children's Hospital. Dr. Landers noted a lot of fluid in her inner ear and said our best option was to do surgery for tubes along with an adenoidectomy. There was some question about whether this "hearing loss" might be affecting her speech, so we agreed to the procedure.

Shortly before Britlyn turned two, we saw her neurologist again. At this point, he had her pegged at being an entire year behind in her gross motor and speech. Along with not talking, she was also not walking. Her reaching and grasping were getting stronger, and though she could crawl and finally sit, her sweet little legs would not do what they were supposed to do. Her small stature was a blessing because we had to carry her everywhere. Britlyn had phenomenal physical therapists. Miss Patti came to our house each week, and Miss Sue utilized the amazing equipment at SPOT. Both ladies were instrumental in helping Britlyn become physically stronger. However, they saw the value in adding yet another specialist, so we began seeing an orthopedic doctor when Britlyn turned two. This doctor felt that Britlyn's progress was good and that nothing anatomically was holding her back. Around this time, Britlyn started using a walker whenever she could, even though she was still not strong enough to use it for long periods of time.

A couple of months after Britlyn turned two, we reconfigured some things at home. Ironically, I had never had a child try to climb out of their crib, but somehow, Britlyn had mastered it. Because of her shaky mobility, we knew we had to figure out a safer way for her to sleep, as flopping out of a crib was not a viable option. It was time for her to move into a toddler bed, but she still needed around-the-clock supervision. She said goodbye to sharing a room with Jakely, and we moved her downstairs with Maci. Although a great sleeper as an infant, we were finding that sleep was becoming a big issue for her. She would often wake at night and need someone to help her fall back asleep. Within a few months, sleep had become such a problem that we were consulting a sleep doctor, and her journey with nightly sleep meds ensued.

When Britlyn was fourteen months old, she received her first pair of glasses. She was adorable! Her eyes were still crossed, however, and even though she could see okay, she began seeing an ophthalmologist as part of her vision journey. We knew she would need surgery to uncross her eyes at some point. A year later, Dr. Ballard was the surgeon who performed the strabismus surgery, which was a great success. She was less sensitive to light, and she was also able to keep her eyes open for longer periods.

We have always wondered if the eye surgery would provide the missing link to her inability to walk because around the time of her surgery, something clicked for Britlyn, and she began to find her stride. By February 2013, at the age of two, she was walking ninety percent of the time, and by that summer, she was fully walking, albeit in a rather wonky manner. Obviously, we were thrilled. The early intervention had made a difference, and our girl was killing it. Speech was still a struggle, however, so I was faced with the difficult decision to advocate for what was best for Britlyn. Her outside speech therapist was a new graduate and would often ask me what I thought about what she was having Britlyn do. I remember thinking that if I knew how to get my daughter to speak, I would have already done it. The teacher's heart in me wanted to give this new girl a chance, but I also knew this was a pivotal time in the process, so I needed to do what was best. And, although Britlyn's demeanor is charming and sweet, she had limits about who she would respond to and work with. We had to make a change, and Miss Jody was the answer. She was able to get Britlyn over the nonverbal hump. By the fall of 2013, Britlyn was using words and could understand speech enough to communicate in her own way. She had yet to fully take off with actually speaking in full sentences, but the progress affirmed the difficult choice of switching therapists.

Even without words and despite Britlyn's many challenges, there is just something contagious about this girl. So many people were praying for her and our family as we continued down the exhausting and uncertain road with our unique daughter. Most people adored Britlyn, but Max is the one who has always had the softest spot in his heart for her. As the oldest child, Max had extra responsibilities at home during this time. He loved to come to her appointments and was always super helpful. Throughout it all, they developed an unbelievably special bond. Because of their connection and because sleep was becoming more of an issue for Britlyn, she responded best to Max helping her get to sleep and stay asleep. The boys had a triple bunk bed in their room, and Max slept on the lowest bunk, which was basically at floor level. We moved a twin mattress into the room right next to his bed, and for the next four years, Max not only put Britlyn to bed each night but also helped her get back to sleep if she woke up in the night. Obviously, their connection is on another level—such a sacrifice of love. Their bond continued to be a blessing because life as we knew it with Britlyn was about to change drastically.

RISING CONFLICT

Throughout this transition for our family, we continued to homeschool the kids. As an advocate for homeschooling in our community, I often tell people the best lessons are not from textbooks. Homeschooling allows us to expose our kids to so many different things, and some days, just learning to run a home, cook a meal, or do laundry are their lessons. Even more than what can be learned by those daily tasks is the chance to learn about life. Often, the best curriculum is found in interacting with people, those we encounter outside our home, and, in our case, the many people who came into our home.

The many therapists and teachers involved with Britlyn through the Birth to Three program became very special to us. At times, it felt like an interruption to our school day, but mostly, we learned to embrace it as a learning experience. Often, Miss Darcee, Miss Patti,

Miss Sue, or Miss Margaret allowed the other kids to help work with Britlyn, which became a highlight for them. We all learned that some kids with special needs must have help to learn even the most basic things: grasping a toy, isolating and poking a finger, shaking a rattle, developing strength in their core, and making and repeating sounds. So many things to learn, so many lessons in the process. All of it was an experience the kids would have missed if they had been away at school during the day. Each interaction would have felt intrusive had we not collectively developed relationships with these people who had become so dear to us.

The hard part about the Birth to Three program is that it ends when the child turns three. We continued outside therapy, but the in-home portion was finished. For Britlyn to continue getting services, she would have to enroll at the public school. When we started homeschooling, we agreed to do whatever was best for each kid. It was time to see if that decision would stick. Obviously, Britlyn would get more one-on-one attention if we sent her to school, and because we attributed her current successes to early interventions, discontinuing things seemed foolish.

On November 3, 2013, Britlyn went to school for the first time. She went four days a week for two hours a day. Riding the bus was an option for her, but my mama heart could not give up that much control. We dropped her off and picked her up daily, Monday through Thursday.

She quickly fell into a nice routine and absolutely loved everything about school.

At the end of the school year, she was referred to a neuropsychologist who tested her abilities cognitively, emotionally, and mentally. We received good feedback that helped us better understand the mind of Britlyn. At that point, she had not yet received an ADHD diagnosis and was not showing any signs of autism, even though her neurologist predicted that both would surface in the future.

THE DOCTORS PREDICTED SHE WOULD PROBABLY NEVER WALK AND MOST LIKELY WOULD NEVER TALK.

Britlyn returned to school in the fall of 2014 and continued with short days. We did allow her to take the bus right after lunch, but we still picked her up at the end of her school day. Around the time she turned four, she was tapping into her speech, and it was such a blessing to communicate fully with our girl. We still did outside speech with Miss Jody and began food therapy and physical therapy closer to home back in Monticello. This time, we went to Capernaum Pediatric Therapy. Appointments had become a consistent part of our weeks, and we did not know life without them.

When Britlyn was first diagnosed with her genetic disorder, the doctors predicted she would probably never walk and most likely would never talk. At four years old, Britlyn not only walked, she ran. She skipped. She jumped. She did somersaults. She could ride a bike with training wheels. At four years old, Britlyn could talk enough that we could understand her. She could spell her name. She could count to ten. She had defied the odds, and this girl who was once diagnosed as failure to thrive was more than thriving—she was living her best life! Every ounce of intervention, every therapy appointment, every minute of sacrifice to get her what she needed was beyond worth it. It was a family effort, and it was an experience that grew us in patience, in love, and in connection with each other. We weathered this challenge together and became stronger because of it. Even though Britlyn could walk and talk, there would be more obstacles to overcome in her future. Yet, she had made huge steps toward a high-functioning life, and that was worth celebrating!

> IT WAS A FAMILY EFFORT, AND IT WAS AN EXPERIENCE THAT GREW US IN PATIENCE, IN LOVE, AND IN CONNECTION WITH EACH OTHER.

The next step for Britlyn was kindergarten. After witnessing all of her success, our plan was to bring her home to school with us at that stage. That was the plan. That was OUR plan. God had a different idea. We would soon see that the life we had lived the previous four years was a precursor to what was coming. Things were about to get really shaken up because now that Britlyn was ready for kindergarten and Jakely had just turned four, a new sibling entered our story.

Jensyn Marcella was born September 9, 2016. Our largest age gap. Our best blessing. Our hardest challenge. Our last child. The girl who quickly became our everything.

BABY GIRL DRAMA

"Mom, when do I get a big girl bed?"

I remember this question well. I also recall feeling some mom guilt that the question had been asked at all. Jakely was three and a half, more than old enough to kick the crib to the curb and move into a big girl bed. Normally, another baby on its way would prompt the change, the decision to swap out beds made for me. Not so this time. We had waited so long between babies at this point that our sweet daughter had to beg for a bed.

"Yes, Jakely. You are absolutely old enough to have a new bed. Let's get out the toddler bed and change things up in your room," I said.

It was December 2015, the perfect time for a new room setup. I asked Chris to dismantle the crib so we could situate the toddler bed. Perhaps it was because this crib had been used by all seven of our children, or maybe it was because we had never really taken down the crib between kids, but when we went to collapse the frame, it fell apart. Irreparably apart. Because our babies usually came a little closer together and because Jakely was over three years old, we took this as our sign that perhaps God was finished adding to our crew. Either way, this crib would not hold another baby, and it had more than served its purpose, so we got rid of it.

Removing the crib ignited a spark in me. It suddenly seemed like the Salvevold Seven would be it for us, so I eliminated more "baby" stuff from our house. I donated maternity clothes and sold baby toys. We rearranged the room that Brinkley and Jakely shared to make it fit for two little girls and their big girl beds. It felt so weird to have a room without a crib or a changing table or a diaper genie—it was bittersweet to say goodbye to these things that had been staples in our home for so long. Yet it felt like our new reality. We really did believe God had completed our family at this time.

I WAS FORTY-TWO, AND I WAS PREGNANT. SURPRISE! SERIOUSLY?

And then it was January 2016. I was forty-two, and I was pregnant. Surprise! Seriously? I had just gotten rid of all things baby! Oh, the sense of humor our God has! Of course, Chris and I were thrilled after the initial shock, but we had no idea how the kids would react. Even after the five crazy years we had just endured with Britlyn's diagnosis and therapies, and with the birth of Jakely thrown in the mix, we had somehow fallen into a routine. We had the life we were currently living figured out—sort of. However, despite not knowing how a new baby would be received, we were not deterred from trying to find a creative way to tell the kids.

Tate turned nine on January 24. Typically, whenever someone has a birthday, we take turns telling the birthday person what we love about them and share affirmations for them. It was Tate's turn in the hot seat. After each person took the opportunity to tell Tate how funny and compassionate and sensitive and loving he is, Chris and I knew we had a captive audience.

"So, it's Tate's birthday today, right?" Chris said. "Whose birthday is next?"

Collectively, the kids shouted out who would be celebrated next.

"Mom is next," Max said. "And then it's me."

"I'm after Max," Chris said.

"Then it's Maci, and who's after Maci?" I asked.

"Me!" shouted Jakely. "It's me!"

"That's right, Jakely," Chris replied. "Then who?"

"It's me," Tygen chimed in.

"No," Chris said. "That's not right."

"Yes, it is!" Tate screamed. "It's Tygen."

"Mommy, Tygen *is* next," confirmed Brinkley.

"No," said Chris, looking at me. "I don't think it's Tygen."

"It is too Tygen," said Max.

"It used to be Tygen," I said, knowingly. "It's not Tygen anymore."

The kids were getting agitated that we were not going in the correct order and were skipping Tygen, whose birthday had always followed Jakely's.

Finally, Maci picked up on what was happening, "Wait! What? You're pregnant? Seriously? Like actually?" There was no excitement in her questions. She just asked them. I saw the wheels spinning as she tried to regulate this new information.

"Wait. I think we're getting pranked," Tygen said. "We're totally getting pranked."

Meanwhile, Max sat up in his chair and faced me. "Ah, hang on. Hang on, hang on, hang on. Wait a minute. Are you serious? Please tell me this is true!" I nodded. "YES!" He screamed and proceeded to jump around the living room in true Max excitement.

The other kids talked over each other as they tried to get all the details. I held Brinkley on my lap, and Tate sat next to me. Brinkley screamed and hugged my neck. In his excitement, Tate began to jump on the couch and then on me. Tygen joined Max, jumping around in celebration with a belly bump and some fist pumps. Jakely broke out in crazy loud sobs and would not even look at me as Maci did her best to console her. Britlyn was oblivious to what was happening but started crying because it seemed like the thing to do. Once Jakely settled down, we could assess that the issue was that she was not okay giving up her position as the baby of the family. In her defense, she had held the role for the longest time. We had anticipated a mixed review, but we had no idea how this reality would hit each kid. It did not take long for them to accept the news and start getting excited for their baby sibling to come.

Since I was an older mom, my regular family doctor, who had delivered our five previous babies, decided that it would be better for me to see an OBGYN instead this time. He knew he would have to "farm me out" for extra ultrasounds and such, so he turned me loose from the beginning. It was on me to find a new doctor and one willing to accept the challenge of an older pregnant mama who had already had seven other babies. Soliciting help from a friend, I began to see her doctor in St. Cloud, which meant I would also deliver in St. Cloud, which was new to me. Overall, my pregnancy was uneventful. I definitely felt older with this one, but other than feeling exhausted and struggling to keep up with life, things felt pretty much the same as my previous pregnancies.

Of course, the kids wanted to know the gender of the baby, and in the past, we had always taken the family with us to the ultrasound so we could find out together. This time, Maci had drivers' education during the appointment time, so we decided to do a gender reveal just for the kids instead. Gender reveal parties were not a thing when we were pregnant with our older kids, but they were gaining popularity around this time. After finding out the gender, Chris and I visited the party store, where they helped us fill the black balloons with the appropriate colored confetti. We took the balloons home to the kids, anticipating a fun reveal. The kids lined up along the banister in our dining room, armed with a balloon and a thumb tack. On the count of three, they were supposed to prick their balloons simultaneously to rain out the confetti. In true large-family fashion, Brinkley jumped the gun and popped hers first. As soon as the kids saw the first piece of pink glitter floating out of the balloon, pandemonium ensued. The big kids were not surprised, but they were ticked Brinkley had popped her balloon early. The little girls were thrilled to see that they were getting another sister, and Tate immediately burst into tears. Most of the family had hoped to even things up with a boy, but Tate absolutely had his heart set on another brother.

Sheesh! This baby was causing so many emotions, and she had not even been born. And, although there was no need to pop the rest of the balloons, naturally, each kid wanted their turn. So, after I wiped away Tate's tears, I got to mop up the rest of the pink confetti. Sure, mixing things up with another boy might have been fun, but I was thrilled the ultrasound had shown a healthy baby. That was the only reveal I needed.

PLOT TWIST

The rest of my pregnancy was uneventful, and we were doing what we could to prepare for her arrival. We borrowed a crib from a friend and rearranged Brinkley and Jakely's room one more time to accommodate another girl in the space. Our home was not very big, but we made it work. We had made it through another summer, and a new homeschool year was upon us. Since there was always a time of transition whenever a new baby joins our family, we decided it might be best for Britlyn to stay in public school through kindergarten, bringing her home for sure for first grade. School was planned; everything was in order at home. It was time for baby to arrive.

The delivery room is such a special place for our family. In fact, Chris and I have always been open to sharing the labor and delivery experience with others. My mom was there to witness the births of Max and Maci. When I had

Tygen, we were at a new hospital in a new town, so we needed my mom to stay with our other kids. My friend, Gretchyn, was interested in seeing a birth, so we invited her to join us when Tate was born. As our kids got older, Chris and I decided we wanted to give them the opportunity to be with us if they wanted to when I delivered one of their siblings.

After clearing it with the doctor, Max and Maci were the first to take us up on our offer. They and my mom were with us when Brinkley was born. Max was ten, and Maci was eight at the time. Maci loved every part of it, but Max? "Um, it was a bit much, Mom," he said. And he never chose to watch another sibling's birth. Maci, on the other hand, was also there for Britlyn's birth along with my mom and my friend Katrina, and Maci and Mom would have been at Jakely's, but Jakely came too early in the morning, so everyone missed that one. Now, over four years later, it was time for the kids to decide who wanted to be in the delivery room to see this sister be born. Maci was a sure thing. Brinkley was all in. Tygen thought being in the room sounded doable (he just didn't want to "see" anything). Tate, ever the queasy kid, had zero desire to be in that environment. Britlyn and Jakely were too little, and Max? "Naw. I'm good, Mom."

Our unofficial family rule is that the kids can join us in the delivery room once I get my epidural. After having the first three babies without an epidural or pain meds, I assumed I would always deliver the same way. However, after Tygen was born, my doctor actually suggested that I try an epidural the next time for my husband's sake. Really? For my husband? What in the world? He explained that it is so difficult for a husband to see his wife in so much pain. Hmmm. I'm not sure I buy that logic, but then a friend told me that getting an epidural is like going to Target and coming home with a baby. Now, that sounded like something I could wrap my brain around! So, with Tate I gave the epidural a go, and I realized my friend was right—it was life-changing, for sure. After having experienced birth both ways, I continued to choose the less painful route. Not sure if I would actually liken it to shopping at Target, but it has made it possible for my kids to have memories they might not have otherwise been able to have.

As my pregnancy was coming to its end, I was naturally getting bigger and bigger. Of course, my "geriatric pregnancy" required weekly ultrasounds at this point. Having a new doctor was not an issue, but specific questions about this pregnancy might have been more easily answered had he had a frame of reference from my other ones. Most of my babies averaged eight pounds. Tygen and Britlyn were around seven pounds, and Jakely tipped the scales at nine pounds. Since Jakely was the baby born before this one, the doctor believed I was carrying a ten-pound baby. He suggested I get induced at least one week early. As a lover of dates and numbers, September 9 sounded perfect. And it was a Friday. Chris's day off is Friday. The planner in me loved this part of the induction!

Dr. Stocker requested that I be at the hospital bright and early on our new due date. Chris and I walked into a gorgeous room overlooking the lake in St. Cloud. We were given the delivery suite! It was the biggest room I had ever delivered in, and we were more than ready to meet our girl. The first order of business was to break my water. When the doctor broke my water, the nurse could hardly keep up with how much fluid I had. After saturating four large bath towels, my nurse said she had never seen that much amniotic fluid and Dr. Stocker agreed that it was an insane amount. Being competitive, I remember feeling a bit of pride in what I had produced! In hindsight, perhaps this should have tipped us off that there would be more in store than usual, but we thought nothing of it then. My belly was visibly deflating right before my eyes, and when I got up to use the bathroom, I could already see my feet past my belly. I had lost so much fluid!

After breaking my water, things progressed well, and all seemed on track for an uneventful delivery. They started the Pitocin, and the contractions began. Around noon, they offered me my epidural, and I took it. Since Chris admittedly does not do well with blood and needles and is not interested in watching me get my epidural, he met my mom, Maci,

Tygen, and Brinkley to get lunch. Typically, after I get my epidural, it still takes several hours before I get the urge to push, so I was not anticipating anything different this time. They returned from lunch around 12:30, and all placed bets on what time baby girl would come. Some said within an hour or two; others said she would not come until later in the evening. Weirdly, about thirty minutes later, I felt the pressure indicative of delivery. I called the nurse in to check me, and it turns out I was complete. Baby was coming. The doctor was at his clinic across town so the intern was on duty, but this mama did not want an intern. Fortunately, Dr. Stocker made it back to the hospital just in time, and after pushing through two contractions, Jensyn Marcella was born at 1:11 p.m.

As soon as Dr. Stocker put Jensyn on my chest, we could see something wasn't quite right. She was gray. She was not crying. She was not even close to the ten pounds they had predicted she would be. She was tiny. She was not thriving. In no time, the room was all hands on deck, and Jensyn was whisked away from me and put into an isolette. It felt like an eternity before we finally heard the glorious sound of her sweet little cry. Though weak and somewhat ineffective, it was the sound our hearts were hinging on to make sure that she was with us. The weird thing about this is that nothing was traumatic about her birth. She did not get stuck. The cord was not wrapped around her neck. There were no issues

"THIS LITTLE GIRL HAS A GENETIC DISORDER."

with her delivery. Hers was the quickest, easiest, least dramatic delivery I had ever had. But she was struggling. And we had no idea what was wrong.

Ironically, I was induced a week early because the doctor feared I was delivering a big baby, but Jensyn was not big at all. In fact, she was my teeniest baby at just six pounds, eight ounces. And she was only eighteen and a half inches long—so tiny! Once things were stabilized with Jensyn, they moved us from our delivery suite to our postpartum room. By this time, the rest of the siblings and grandparents had joined us to meet our newest member. All were taking turns snuggling Jensyn, and we were excited to go home soon as a family of ten. Because we were in St. Cloud, Jensyn's pediatrician was not the one on rounds. I do not remember the name of the doctor who came to check on her, but I will always remember his gruff and abrupt bedside manner as he told us things about our newborn daughter we will never forget. As he examined her, he listed off her issues:

"Her toes are crossed, and her fingers are too long."

"Her ears are crumpled, pitted, and triangular in shape."

"Her forehead is big, and her eyes are too far apart."

"She does not have much of a cry."

"This little girl has a genetic disorder."

This little girl has a genetic disorder? Not only did we not appreciate how the doctor delivered his suggested diagnosis, but we also hated that he shared it so cavalierly in front of our other kids. Things did not register with the younger kids, but the big kids heard it loud and clear. The vibe in the room went from excited to uncomfortable, and we could not wait for this doctor to finish his "exam" and leave. When he did, Chris looked at me with a questioning glance, to which I replied, "She has a genetic disorder? We already have one of those." Recognizing that Chris and I might need some time alone to absorb this news, our parents took the rest of the kids home.

At this point, we knew Jensyn had some pretty significant jaundice. Because her delivery was so quick, she had a huge, nasty bruise on the back of her head. She also was not eating well and had dropped to five pounds, eleven ounces. The jaundice and the eating struggles kept us at the hospital for five days before she was finally stable enough for us to join the rest of the family at home.

During this extra time at the hospital, Chris and I did what we could to wrap our brains around everything. As we processed what this might mean for our family and ultimately for Jensyn, we ugly cried together, we prayed for answers, and we just soaked up all of the snuggles we could get when Jensyn was not under the bilirubin lights or trying to figure out how to nurse. I had been officially discharged from the hospital on day three, but they allowed me to stay in the room with Jensyn while we waited for her to get stronger. Because I was no longer a patient in the hospital, Chris would get take-out for our meals. One time, it took longer than usual for him to return with the food, and he shared that he had found himself just driving around St. Cloud as he wept and cried out to God for answers on behalf of his new daughter and our family. After the five years we had just gone through with Britlyn, this seemed like an absurdity, a cruel joke, and for sure, something we could not fully comprehend. How could we be embarking on this special needs genetic journey once again? We had far more questions than answers, and much like when we first learned about Britlyn's diagnosis, we felt abruptly thrown back into the deep waters with absolutely no idea how to even begin to swim, much less stay afloat. Depleted. Defeated. Yet unquestionably devoted to our sweet baby girl!

SUDDENLY SICK

Once we got home, I did my best to transition things back to normal for my family. Every time we bring home a new baby, there is a time of chaos and crazy, but even though Jensyn was an easy baby and a fantastic sleeper, she was not eating well. I would try to nurse her, but she struggled to latch on. Instead, I pumped around the clock, and we bottle-fed her breast milk. It was our hope that as she got stronger and bigger she would eventually figure out breastfeeding.

Being a great sleeper is obviously a goal for any baby, but much like Britlyn, Jensyn did not seem to have appropriate hunger cues and was too sleepy overall. Chris and I had to make sure we got up every few hours so that I could pump and he could wake her up and give her a bottle. This, coupled with the extra days in the hospital and the emotional drain of all the things, made for some pretty exhausted parents.

Those first few days at home were busy. Jensyn had doctor checkups, the kids and I had our homeschool co-op, and we had the usual stuff to do around the house. We had only been home for three days when Jensyn got her first cold. Her nose was stuffy, and this obviously hindered her ability to eat well. Believing maybe we had taken her out too much or pushed her too hard, we figured she would fight through this cold and would soon be better. Yet four days after Jensyn was discharged initially, we found ourselves back in the hospital, and this hospital would soon become our home away from home.

I will never forget that day. Chris and I had been invited to the wedding of a former youth girl. Since Jensyn was not feeling well, I sent Chris without me, and he took Maci as his plus-one. The kids and I were tending to Jensyn, and because she was bottle fed, they would all fuss to feed her. Brinkley and Tate both tried a bottle, but Jensyn had no interest. Jensyn was sleepy, like usual, but eventually woke up a little bit. I decided I would try to feed her. I was so afraid she was getting dehydrated. She was finally hungry, and she sucked down two ounces. Immediately after she finished the bottle, she went limp in my arms. Tate and Max both pointed out that her color was changing—she was pale and turning blue, and I feared she was not breathing. I knew I had to take her in.

When I called Chris, who was still at the wedding, he said I should wait for him to get home and go to the emergency department (ED) with me. I told him he had until I got her in the car seat and buckled into the car to get home otherwise I would leave without him. He got home just in time, and we made our first trip to the emergency room in Monticello. In hindsight, we probably should have called 911, but the idea of an ambulance scared me even though I knew she needed help desperately.

Upon arrival at the hospital, the nurse agreed that Jensyn seemed to have a cold. Since Jensyn was acting hungry again, we gave her another bottle while waiting for the doctor. Her oxygen immediately dipped below 77 (a normal oxygen level is in the 90s), and both the nurse and doctor rushed in to tell us to stop feeding her. Because Jensyn struggled to breathe through her nose, I cut off her oxygen supply while trying to feed her. At this point, everything kicked into high gear. They whisked Jensyn into a trauma room, tried to get her temperature back up (it had fallen below 96 degrees), and did what they could to prepare her for the NICU ambulance, which was in transit from Children's Hospital. Jensyn needed an IV for fluids, but because she was so small and so dehydrated, they could not find a vein in the foot, arm, or hand. I was the lucky one to hold her as they put one in her sweet little head. They also did a chest X-ray and needed to draw some blood for labs. They could not find a vein to draw the needed blood. At one point, the doctor assured me they had everything they needed ready to resuscitate her if it came to that. It was then that I took a step back. I remember looking at my precious baby girl lying there helpless, fragile, and so very sick, and I realized I would do absolutely anything for her—whatever it would take to save her life.

Even though we had no idea what to expect when the ambulance arrived, we were grateful she was being taken to Children's. They understand children, and the nurses and EMTs who came to pick up our daughter did what they could to put our minds at ease. They wrapped up Jensyn and put her into a portable incubator and then suggested I take a picture so that we would forever remember her in this unique mode of travel. I had somehow held it together until this point, but right after I took the photo, I lost it. Pastor Patrick, our senior pastor at the time, came to pray with us as I ugly cried. It was difficult to see Jensyn so sick and to not know what would happen to her.

Chris and I were not allowed to go with Jensyn in the ambulance because the NICU had sent a large team of nurses to watch over her. They suggested we follow behind, and we were more than willing to do that. At this point, they only had the lights on and were hurrying to get Jensyn to the hospital. Chris was able to keep up pretty well, and it wasn't until we were about a mile away from the hospital that we heard the sirens start. This changed things for us because we had not heard any sirens before, so we assumed something must have happened en route. By the time we got checked in

WE HAD NO IDEA AT THIS TIME HOW VITAL THIS COMMUNITY OF PRAYER WARRIORS WOULD BECOME.

and up to the NICU, Jensyn was already in her room and doing much better. She looked rough—she was hooked up to lots of wires and tubes, and she had the tiniest cannula in her nose to give her much-needed oxygen— but we knew she was in good hands. Not only did we immediately love our NICU doctor and nurses, but we had also already texted our church and all our family and friends, who we knew were storming the gates of heaven on our behalf. We had no idea at this time how vital this community of prayer warriors would become because we did not have a clue what was in store for us or Jensyn.

The day was September 17, 2016. This was nine days after Jensyn joined our family. This was her first ambulance ride, her first ICU stay, and her first exposure to the medical community that would soon become like family to us. And as we reached out for prayer, as we cried out to God, as our family rallied to support each other in this new uncertain chapter of our story, and because our only wish was to see our sweet baby girl get better, this was the first time that I ended my entry in Jensyn's journal with "Whatever it takes . . . ."

PROVEN PROGNOSIS

Weekends, we would soon learn, are quiet days in the hospital. The doctors and nursing staff are there to meet the patient's needs and to keep everyone comfortable before the busyness of Monday hits. Jensyn was taken to Children's late on a Saturday, so Sunday was a time for us to acclimate to our new space. Because of the sterile nature of this unit, we were not allowed to eat in the rooms. NICU rooms have no bathrooms, and although we were able to sleep on the makeshift couch bed, we were quickly introduced to the luxury of the Ronald McDonald House.

The Ronald (as it is affectionately called by those who frequently stay there) has individual rooms for parents and families. It also has a lounge area with a television, a workout room, a laundry room, and a full pantry/kitchen that is available for use all day. As we were touring this facility that houses families with sick children, I recall feeling as if we were in a twilight zone of sorts. Its lavishness felt otherworldly and somewhat out of place, being connected to the sterility of a hospital right outside its doors. And how could it possibly be part of our story that our daughter was so sick and fragile that we would be in this position at all? How long would we be in need of accommodations such as these? As nice as it was to have a bed and a shower, it was not easy to leave Jensyn's bedside. Not being with her every minute was unsettling, but sleep was necessary for us to prepare for the week to come.

Monday brought with it a flurry of specialists who ordered tests and procedures. The first doctor who visited was Dr. Landers. He was the ENT who had done Britlyn's ear tubes and adenoidectomy when she was younger. This was our first hint that perhaps the girls would share more specialists in the future. He was summoned to look at Jensyn's nasal cavities and to scope her throat. The concern was a blockage or anomaly might be causing her issues. Everything looked good upon examination, but he ordered a head ultrasound and requested that we redo a hearing test in the coming months.

Next to weigh in on things was the doctor we were most curious to see but also the one we hoped would find nothing wrong: Dr. Bhambhani, the geneticist.

Immediately, he had concerns about Jensyn's unique features, similar concerns to the pediatrician who had first pointed things out to us in St. Cloud. We were grateful his delivery of her list of "issues" was offered with sensitivity and care. He pointed out her long fingers, her equally long, curvy toes, and her cute, little crumpled ears. However, the most astonishing thing he did was take Jensyn's fisted hand and uncurl her fingers. "She has three lines instead of two on the backs of her fingers," he said. "This alone tells us all we need to know." We were amazed that just looking at the backs of her itty-bitty fingers was enough for him to know something was fundamentally off.

Dr. Bhambhani ordered blood work for the chromosomal issue and requested a renal ultrasound and a heart echocardiogram, and he agreed with the already-ordered ultrasound of her head. He also suggested that I get my blood tested to determine whether or not I was the genetic carrier. It was clear that what had started out with us thinking that our daughter had simply gotten sick and was in the hospital needing extra support was becoming something much more. We began to see that Jensyn's future was going to be a journey of investigating and learning and deciphering another genetic disorder, because unlike Britlyn whose issues were mostly developmental in nature, we had no clue what was making Jensyn as sick as she was. We no longer believed Jensyn had merely gotten a cold. In fact, it became crystal clear that Jensyn was actually fighting for her life.

The ultrasounds, bloodwork, and all the ordered tests were done within the next few days. Some of the results were more instantaneous than others, and we were pleased to learn that all the ultrasounds were normal at the time. The heart echo revealed an atrial septal defect (ASD), which in Jenysn's case was a small hole in her heart. The cardiologist was unconcerned because this often happens in babies, and they often close on their own. This had been our experience with Brinkley when she was a baby, so we were not concerned about this now for Jensyn. It was a relief that many of the test results were returning normal, and we already knew that genetic test results would take a little longer. Jensyn seemed to be making improvements overall, and the final thing that needed to happen before we could take her home was for her not to need oxygen. She continued to have so much congestion that it was impossible even to trial her off the nasal cannula for any time. Significantly, her oxygen would dip too low when she was asleep, and her pulse-oximeter machine would alarm the nurses.

After being in the hospital for four days, Jensyn was still not bottling well. In spite of what the ENT said, there was still some question about her ability to swallow. We met with an occupational therapist, which marked the next step on her challenging and uncertain feeding journey. The OT worked with us for several feeding times and wondered about reflux. At this point, it was not clear whether swallowing was the actual issue, but it was evident that eating exhausted Jensyn, and we seemed to be fighting a losing battle. However, since eating is often a developmental habit, we believed we just needed to keep working with Jensyn and that, eventually, she would get it. She weighed six pounds and five ounces at this point, so we were thrilled that she seemed to be moving in the right direction.

After five days in the NICU, Jensyn was finally strong enough not to need oxygen support. The tubes and wires and things that just a few days prior were needed to sustain her had all been stripped away. It seemed to us that Jensyn had made it over another hurdle and that we would finally be able to take her home and finish nursing her back to full strength. Although Chris's parents had been able to be at home with the other kids, Chris had returned to the house for a couple of nights to do what he could to establish normalcy for the rest of the family. When he came back to the hospital to check in with me, we were both excited when the doctor said Jensyn was being discharged that day. It was news to me, and since Chris did not know he was coming back to take us home, the kids were not expecting it either. We decided it would be fun to surprise them.

Finally, we got Jensyn buckled up and ready to go for our one-hour trip home. As we got closer to Becker, I thought it would be fun to do a Facebook Live, capture the surprise for our kids, and update everyone on Jensyn. At this point, only Maci had Facebook. I was hoping that she would not see I had gone live, but it was not long before she jumped on. I pleaded with her to keep our surprise a secret. When we got home, Chris pulled into the driveway, and in her excitement, Maci rushed out to greet us, with Max following. As thrilled as they were to see Jensyn, I think they were equally relieved to have me back home. I remember going into the house and calling out to the other kids. "Hey! Where is everyone? Mama needs a hug!" The rest of the crew scrambled upstairs from the basement, and I will remember that moment for the precious reunion that it was.

It was wonderful to be home over the weekend, and Jensyn finally made her debut at church. Although many of our church family had visited us while we were in the NICU, it was great to see everyone and thank them for praying for us. Max and Maci were on the worship team, and I recall being proud to be there with my entire family. It felt like maybe we were getting back on track, and I was excited for a normal week ahead. On Monday, Jensyn had her two-week well-check appointment, and her weight was up to six pounds, nine ounces. Her pediatrician was hopeful that I would be able to resume breastfeeding soon. We also had a decent homeschool day.

And then Tuesday happened. I was downstairs in our homeschool room working with the kids when my phone buzzed beside me. The caller ID was one that I did not recognize, but my gut told me to answer. Although I was expecting this call, I was not prepared for the news I would receive. It was the nurse calling from Dr. Bhambhani's office. They had Jensyn's results. "Trisomy 5," she divulged. I tuned out everything that was said after that. Sadness overwhelmed me. The pediatrician from St. Cloud—the doctor who was so brash, bold, and abrasive—was right. "This little girl has a genetic disorder," he had said. And now we had the results to prove it.

DISORDER DEFINED

S till reeling from Jensyn's diagnosis, I remember thinking that I would give myself some time to grieve and cry, but then I would dig deep and find the strength to do whatever was needed to help Jensyn thrive despite this twist. We had done it with Britlyn, and we would do it again with Jensyn. I was filled with a fresh resolve, and I knew that even though we did not know what we were up against, we would figure things out along the way. Meanwhile, we had to think about our other children— Tygen was turning twelve!

Two days after we received the call regarding Jensyn's diagnosis and six days after being discharged from the NICU, we went out as a family to celebrate Tygen's birthday. He chose Val's Restaurant, a fun outdoor burger joint in St. Cloud, and we had a great time together. When we got home later that night, I fed Jensyn her bottle. She immediately vomited the entire amount, turned gray again, and went limp in my arms. I called out to Chris, and this time, I did not even bother to put her in the car seat. I scooped her up in my arms and crawled into the back of our fifteen-passenger van. I willed Chris to go faster as we drove her back to the emergency room in Monticello, about fifteen minutes away. Again, we probably should have called 911, but we somehow believed that we could get her the help she needed faster than waiting for help to come to us. Here is an excerpt from the journal entry I wrote for Jensyn later that night:

October 2, 2016

> *After I gave you a bottle tonight, you gagged and threw it all back up. Then you filled your diaper more than I have ever seen you fill it. When I looked at you, you were gray and limp. I knew you were not breathing well again. I called for Dad to come see you, and we KNEW we had to get you to the ED! We thought about calling 911, but Dad drove instead. I held you in the back seat. Oh, sweet baby, you were not doing well. When we got into the van, I bumped your head on the back of the front seat. You made a face like you were going to cry, but no sound came out. I was so scared that Dad would not make it*

to the hospital in time. I kept moving you and talking to you—I was afraid you would fall asleep and not wake up. We made it to the hospital, and

THE QUESTION REMAINED: NOT EVEN A WHOLE WEEK AT HOME—HOW COULD OUR LITTLE GIRL BE SO SICK AGAIN?

they got you back on oxygen. You perked up a little bit, but they still got the ambulance ready. This time, I rode with you back to Children's. I never thought we would be back here so soon. Such a sad night, but so great that you are going to be fine.

The question remained: not even a whole week at home—how could our little girl be so sick again?

Familiar tubes, wires, and that dreaded nasal cannula were again part of the equation. We had so many questions about why Jensyn was so sick and why she could not seem to get better or stronger. While we were in the NICU this time, we had the opportunity to meet with Dr. Bhambhani and his genetic counselor, Sara. I have said more than once that geneticists operate on a different level of brain power. They are so stinking smart that it is nearly impossible for them to simplify things enough for us common folk to understand. Thank God for genetic counselors because they are the perfect bridge between the brilliance of the doctor and the rest of us who are just trying to grasp a fraction of what the doctors are sharing. What we thought we would learn and what we were told were completely different things. Trisomy 5, specifically Trisomy 5p, is extremely rare. We were told that there are only fifty reported cases of this particular Trisomy in the world. Because of this, there is little known about what to expect, but the genetic counselor handed us a packet with information about what they do know. The pages shared why they did the genetic testing—"because of her sister's 10q deletion and because of physical differences noted at birth."

The next page shared the results:

- Jensyn does not have the same 10q deletion that her sister has.
- Jensyn does have Trisomy 5p due to an isochromosome of 5p and one of her fifth chromosomes missing 5p (an isochromosome is a mirror-image abnormal chromosome consisting of two copies of either a short arm or a long arm).

Next, was another list. This list was specific to what individuals with Trisomy 5p typically have:

- Unique facial features
- Heart defects
- Structural renal defects

- Macrocephaly/hydrocephalus/ventriculomegaly
- Frequent respiratory infections
- Developmental delays/intellectual disability
- Seizures

Seeing such a list was daunting. We had already been told about the unique facial features. The hole in her heart had been determined. Renal defects? At this point, her kidney ultrasound was normal. Macrocephaly—in simple terms, this means that an infant's head is bigger than a typical child's head. Although this was not evident in Jensyn as an infant, later in life, her large head caused her to struggle. Hydrocephalus is fluid in the brain that causes the head to swell. This neurological disorder did not affect Jensyn; she also did not have ventriculomegaly. We assumed that she would have developmental and intellectual disabilities as we had already been down that road with her sister. As far as frequent respiratory infections and seizures are concerned, we had no idea at the time of her diagnosis how much these would later affect her life, even though she had already been hospitalized twice for respiratory distress.

Naturally, we had many more questions for Dr. Bhambani and Sara. We asked them about the life expectancy for someone with Trisomy 5p. Because such little information is known, they said there was not enough data to answer that question. We were told that the first year or two would be critical to figure out Jensyn's needs and combat what might come about because of this condition. I also asked if any of this had to do with my age. Did the fact that I gave birth to her at age forty-three play into her diagnosis at all? Dr. Bhambani said that only two trisomies are connected to age—Trisomy 13 and Trisomy 18—so he believed there was no indication that my advanced maternal age was a reason for this condition.

Finally, I absolutely had to hear his thoughts on how one family could have two daughters with completely different genetic disorders. We were told they were not certain whether Jensyn's 5p trisomy was related to Britlyn's 10q deletion. Yet, because there were two instances of genetic disorders, they reiterated their recommendation of parental testing. They believed that testing us would help provide information regarding any future pregnancies I might have. It would also allow them to counsel Jensyn's siblings if we learned they might be at risk of having children with conditions similar to Jensyn or Britlyn. Chris had been tested after Britlyn's diagnosis, but because I had been pregnant with Jakely, I had not been tested at that time. He had only been tested for the 10q deletion, so the recommendation was that we both be tested to see if there was some connection with chromosomes 10 and 5.

We agreed to do the testing. To have one child with a chromosomal abnormality is enough, but to have two warrants a thorough investigation into the cause. Many have wondered whether I had done the genetic testing that was offered to me when I was twelve weeks pregnant with Jensyn. I remember talking extensively with my doctor about the chances of having another child with a genetic disorder, and his response was clear: not only did I have six other healthy and typical children, but I had had a healthy child born after the one with the disorder. I recall him saying that he believed my chances of having another child with a genetic abnormality would be less than one in a million. Based on his counsel, I did not see the need to do the twelve-week bloodwork.

Considering what the genetic testing uncovered with Jensyn and Britlyn, Chris and I went ahead with the testing. We learned that neither Chris nor I are carriers for either of the chromosomal abnormalities in our daughters. They are considered de novo variants—a type of variant present for the first time in a child and not inherited from either parent. De novo variants can occur spontaneously during the formation of the egg or sperm cell or shortly after fertilization. Though grateful that we were not the reason our girls would live a different, more difficult life and equally thankful that our grandchildren would not be at risk of these genetic disorders, this answer was just an answer. Even though these results filled in a few blurry sections of the overall picture, they did nothing to change the course of our daughters' lives.

CONFINED AND CONFUSED

Tygen's birthday was on September 30. Jensyn was discharged from her second ICU stay on October 3. This stay's diagnosis? The rhinovirus. For most people, it is a common cold. For Jensyn, it required being on oxygen and subjecting her nasal passages to suction to eliminate secretions she was unable to get rid of on her own. Fortunately, this was a much shorter stay for us, and again, we anticipated being able to go home and finally resume life together.

However, because of these two hospital stays, Chris and I were strongly encouraged to do infant CPR training. We were also educated on using our pulse-oximeter (pulse-ox) machine. Both of us had taken multiple CPR classes over the years, but it hit us a bit differently when we realized there was a genuine possibility that we might have to actually use it on our infant daughter. It made us listen more attentively and learn all that we could.

Our first night home with the pulse-ox machine was interesting. It brought us some peace of mind but alarmed more than we thought it would. It was difficult to assess what was an emergency and what was not. After two rough nights of alarms, we called Jensyn's neonatologist, Dr. Perdue, who agreed we could lower the settings so that it would not alarm so frequently. We were grateful for her help.

Over the next couple of days, Jensyn had another doctor's appointment to check her weight, and we were thrilled to see that she was seven pounds. Thinking things were finally moving in the right direction, we adjusted our schedule to keep Jensyn home and quarantined as much as possible. She could *not* get sick again. Unfortunately, our attempts did not matter as we found ourselves back in the NICU four days later on October 7. This time, her pulse-ox registered that her oxygen was pretty consistently in the 70s. Once again, I texted Dr. Perdue (Seriously, how many doctors give out their personal phone

THE PAST FEW WEEKS HAD FINALLY CAUGHT UP WITH ME—I WAS EMOTIONALLY DRAINED.

numbers to make themselves available at any time?) After she received my text, Dr. Perdue called me to say that we should take Jensyn back to Children's. This time, she had called ahead, and we were able to drive her there ourselves. They had her room waiting for her when we got there, and thankfully there was a room ready for us at the Ronald as well.

Of course, it was another weekend, and weekends are biding-time days. Although her oxygen was low enough to warrant another stay, she was not as sick this time. This was good because the nurses were able to see what might be contributing to her continued congestion and stuffiness. They believed she was aspirating and refluxing her milk. In order to confirm this, they wanted to do a swallow study. Since it was a weekend, we knew we would need to wait until Monday for the study.

I was still disappointed when I heard we had to wait, and my resolve was fading fast. The past few weeks had finally caught up with me—I was emotionally drained, mentally exhausted, and now physically sick. In fact, I was so sick that I was no good for Jensyn at the hospital. We spent the night in the Ronald, and then Chris talked me into going home with him the next night. Leaving my daughter behind was excruciating. I didn't think I would ever do that, but I agreed that I needed sleep and I was not helping Jensyn's health by exposing her to my illness. So we went home. But only for one night. We were back at the hospital by Monday, ready for Jensyn's swallow test. Because of Jensyn's many needs, we were learning so much. I had never heard of a swallow test, much less seen one done. Jensyn was given a special formula, which we could see on an X-ray. As she swallowed, we could watch where the liquid was going. She did pretty well, but a lot of the formula was going up her nose, which was contributing to her congestion, and it threatened to go down her airway as well. Because of this, Jensyn's feeding team decided to use a thicker formula that consisted of added oatmeal. This meant that she had to stay another twenty-four hours to see how she would tolerate things. Since my breast milk, which I was still pumping, was not going to be needed at this time, the doctors and Chris convinced me to go home and stop by urgent care on the way. I was diagnosed with pneumonia! Nothing about life was easy for us at this time, and after being in the hospital more than we were home during Jensyn's first month of life, it was difficult to see anything but hard in our future.

We did bring Jensyn home the next day and hoped that bottling with the new, thickened formula would be the answer. Yet she did not do as well on it at home as she did when she was at the hospital. It was taking her more than thirty minutes to drink a couple of ounces. Her feeding therapist said this meant she was actually not getting any sustenance at all. When it took that long to eat, she was burning the calories she had just consumed just by continuing to eat. We were beginning to see that a feeding tube could quite possibly be a reality for our girl.

We desperately wanted to avoid the feeding tube, so we did what we could to help Jensyn learn to bottle this new formula well. It saddened me that it did not seem like she would ever be able to breastfeed, and because of my pneumonia, my milk supply dried up. If formula and bottling around the clock were what she needed, we would do it.

As we struggled to feed Jensyn, the insane number of appointments outside the hospital was beginning to increase, and our journey with a pulmonologist began. Because of Jensyn's respiratory issues, we knew we would be working closely with a specialist in this area. We were connected to a nurse practitioner who immediately showed compassion and understanding for what we were going through. I remember being so grateful that she not only attended to Jensyn's needs but she also recognized Chris and I were struggling. Her compassion for both of us was a balm to our exhausted and uncertain souls. It was at this very appointment that she made a declaration that would change my life in a way that I never saw coming.

In our meeting to discuss our concerns for Jensyn, we mentioned that we had a trip coming up. It was a trip to Dallas, Texas, that I had earned from my side hustle selling health and wellness supplements. I recall her dubious expression when we asked her what she thought about taking Jensyn with us. Her response still weirdly haunts me to this day: "You can't take Jensyn on a plane to a different state. In fact, you shouldn't be taking Jensyn anywhere. You should keep her home as much as possible."

We were pretty much already doing that, but we felt we needed clarity on what "anywhere" meant. Chris said, "I am a pastor. Are you implying that we should not even take Jensyn to church?" I thought that was a bizarre question to ask. There was no way we would be told not to go to church!

"Jensyn needs to be kept away from all people," she answered, "and that includes any place where a group of people might be carrying something. You need to realize that when Jensyn gets sick, you *will* be going to the hospital."

I was willing to put parts of life on hold. Not going on my trip was a bummer, and limiting her exposure outside of the house would be difficult, but we would do it. But no church? Church has always been my community of support. I love our church family, and I needed them more than ever right then. This felt surreal, and as it turned out, it led to a deep loss. And in the midst of this unbelievable, unacceptable loss, I was beginning to lose myself.

ONE CHEERIO AT A TIME

J ensyn's feeding issues did not improve on the thickened formula, so we knew the next step would be a feeding tube. At only two months old, it was hard to imagine her undergoing sedating surgery, but at the same time, we knew it was necessary. She was not gaining enough weight or getting bigger. She was only a little over eight pounds at two months old and was still considered failure to thrive. Failure to thrive is traditionally used to describe children who have failed to develop and grow normally. It is commonly used for any child who fails to gain weight or height according to standard medical growth charts. Other issues that flag failure to thrive are that a child does not feed well or has poor sucking, sleeps too much, has a weak cry, has stiff or floppy muscles, or any combination of these things. Needless to say, we did not question this diagnosis.

We met again with her feeding therapy team, and they shared their concerns. Their suggestion was that we go to Children's ED and be admitted for a nasogastric tube (NG tube). An NG tube is placed in the nose or mouth and slid into the stomach. For feedings, a formula is put into the tube so that it can flow directly into the stomach. Our team said that we should be able to get the tube placed and then go home to trial it for a few weeks. When we got to the ED, we learned that they rarely send children home on NG tubes and would never send someone as fragile as Jensyn home on one.

Though the medical staff agreed that Jensyn was a candidate for an actual feeding tube (a tube that is placed in a hole in the stomach to provide nutrition when someone cannot eat or drink by mouth), the surgeons could not do the surgery until the following week. Our visit to the ED was on a Thursday. This meant another weekend stay for our little girl. This also meant more disruption for our kids at home. Being away from home so much was taking a toll on all of us, and I knew a difficult decision needed to be made. Because Jensyn was in good hands and because she was not critically sick, I agreed to go home with Chris and, once again, leave Jensyn at the hospital.

The NICU is built to house long-term patients, so they are equipped to set up cameras for parents who cannot be bedside with their children at all times. This was a comfort to me, albeit a small one. It was wonderful to be home with the rest of the family while also being able to see Jensyn whenever we needed or wanted to. I remember how difficult it was when we saw her on the screen crying, hoping for the nurses to tend to her needs. It yanked on my mama's heart something fierce, but being able to somewhat be in both places at once was a gift.

Being home felt anything but normal, and it was at these moments that I began to hate the expression "finding a new normal." Nothing about life was normal; everything was out of sync and crazy. I did what I could to keep things under control for the other kids while still juggling school, co-op, and Briltyn's continued therapy appointments. Absolutely everything felt out of control in my mind and in my heart, but somehow, we managed to do what we needed to do together to make life work.

After being home for a few days, Chris and I went back to check on Jensyn. We were under the impression that her surgery would take place early in the week, but we found out the surgeon was not available until the end of the week. After cuddling her for a night, I went home to join the rest of the family again. It was just too hard for them to have me gone so much, and Britlyn was celebrating her sixth birthday. I did not want to miss that.

The end of the week arrived, and it was finally time for the feeding tube surgery. Most kids do well with a gastrostomy tube or a G-tube, but Jensyn's team decided she would need a GJ tube (gastrostomy and jejunostomy).

The G-tube goes into the stomach, but the GJ tube goes into both the stomach and the small intestine. The concern was that the G-tube would still cause Jensyn to reflux, and her issues would continue. By bypassing the stomach and going straight into the small intestine, she would be better able to tolerate her feeds.

The surgery went well. Believing what we had been told about the feeding tube only being a temporary solution, we sat through the training on how to work the food pump and how to vent her stomach. So many new things to learn with this child. I was starting to feel overwhelmed, and again I was hit with a sense of drowning in the deep end of a pool with no escape. More new machines at home. Feeding our daughter through a tube. Ordering supplies from a medical supply company. Staying ahead of everything. Too much to process. Too many things to grasp. How were we ever going to keep our heads above water? Would this finally be the life-saving measure our daughter needed to thrive?

It quickly became obvious that we had made the right decision to get Jensyn the feeding tube because she was finally able to get the calories and nutrition she needed to grow, but it caused many more trips to the ER and took us on adventures we will never forget. When the surgeon first puts in a feeding tube, the contraption they use is temporary. For Jensyn, a port was attached to her tummy, and another tube was hooked up to that port, which connected to a bag of formula that was pumped into the stomach or small intestine. This tube was super long, and its only real support was a popsicle stick taped close to the body to limit movement and keep it from falling out. Eventually, this contraption would be replaced by a much more secure button, but the surgical hole had to heal before this better button could be placed. This process often takes months. The tricky part for us was that Jensyn's formula was being pumped into her jejunum (part of the small intestine) instead of the stomach. Because of this, she could not tolerate bolus feeds or large amounts of formula at one time. Instead, she had to be fed on a continuous drip for twenty-three hours a day. I explained to the kids that it was like Jensyn only eating one Cheerio at a time, all day long, instead of ever eating a full bowl of cereal at once. Because she was feeding for so many hours of the day, we were constantly battling her tube and attachments, and things didn't always stay where they were supposed to.

Within the first few weeks of having the tube, we were still trying to figure out how to do all the things. At one point, the tube got clogged, so we had to fix it. The thought of dragging her back to Children's was more than I could bear, so I decided to take her to the ED in St. Cloud. I assumed all hospitals would know what to do. I was wrong. We arrived at 9:30 a.m., and there was some concern about what they needed to do. This lack of confidence should have tipped me off, and their belief that Jensyn needed to be sedated should have definitely given me pause, but we proceeded. By 1:30 p.m., they began the procedure. Something that was supposed to take about fifteen minutes took forty-five minutes. Hindsight was clear.

Either way, the tube was replaced, and Jensyn and I headed home. Later that night, while we were setting up our Christmas tree, Brinkley was holding Jensyn, who was crying and very upset. She was also all wet. As I looked over to where Brinkley was sitting, I noticed Jensyn's new tube lying on the floor, goo oozing out of her belly. Because she was losing fluid, we were unsure of what to do, so we called 911. The paramedics came and capped off her tube and suggested she be taken to Children's to get this new wrinkle ironed out. We decided Chris would stay back with the kids. I did not want to go alone, so Maci agreed to go with me. We followed behind the ambulance, assuming we would get the tube replaced and then return home later that night. Unfortunately, a radiologist was unavailable when we arrived, so they admitted us. At two months old, Jensyn had graduated from the NICU, and we began our journey on a regular hospital floor—with our own bathroom and a TV, a marked improvement over the regulatory feel of the NICU.

The following day, the radiologist was able to replace the tube. When I asked him why they did not sedate Jensyn, he said it was unnecessary. I knew then that, if possible, we would never take Jensyn to any other hospital that did not specialize in children. We had gone to the Monticello ED twice, and they sent us straight to Children's. And our hope that St. Cloud could handle our emergency was proved wrong. It was becoming clear that someone as complex as Jensyn was better off where complicated was dealt with on the daily.

Oh, that feeding tube. It continued to give us issues as we waited for the permanent button to be placed. We were longing for January, which is when that surgery was slated to happen. After a low-key Christmas without any hospital stays, we were hopeful and excited for a new year, but in January, Jensyn had her first seizure and her first urinary tract infection (UTI)—two new things that we would continue to chase throughout this exhausting and uncertain journey.

NEVER-ENDING HICCUPS

"It's like her legs have hiccups," Maci told me when I walked in the door. She had been watching four-month-old Jensyn while I was at a therapy session with Britlyn. Chris was home, too, so we laid Jensyn down and observed her. Sure enough, her legs twitched every so often, and then her arms would join in the twitching. Her entire body would quiver and spasm a bit—repeatedly. Knowing that seizures were a possibility with her condition, we had been on the lookout for this behavior. After a call to her pediatrician, we were advised to take her back to Children's once again.

Unfortunately, since Jensyn was getting another cold and because she did have a bit of a fever, they were not sure if the seizures were linked to that or if she was actually having them because of her condition. Jensyn was admitted and hooked up for the first time to an EEG (electroencephalogram), a test that measures electrical activity in the brain using small metal electrodes attached to the scalp. The multicolored cords are long and flow off the head—we liked to call these wires her rainbow extensions! Dr. Janousek, her neurologist, determined that she was having myoclonic seizures, a type of seizure that causes quick jerking movements, almost like hiccups. Maci's description of what was happening with Jensyn was more medical than she knew! Once diagnosed, Jensyn was given a new med to regulate these movements, and we were sent home.

Jensyn's GJ tube button surgery was scheduled for January 20. In the middle of the night prior to that day, she woke up with a fever of 102.7 and was having seizures. We still opted to take her to the hospital for her surgery, not knowing what they would do. Typically, we had always gone to Children's in Minneapolis, but her GI surgeon had been planning to do the surgery at Children's in St. Paul. Once we met with the anesthesiologist, she declared that there were too many red flags to do the surgery then. This was the first surgery she had canceled in five years. Ugh. We were so bummed to be sent home. We were told to get her healthy and then to reschedule her surgery. With Jensyn being so sick, we were surprised they chose to send us home, but what were our options?

We ran a quick errand on the way home, and by the time we were finished, Jensyn's fever had spiked again and she was abnormally fussy. Not sure how to calm her down, we opted to take her to urgent care at our normal clinic in Monticello. Our family doctor was in. He took one look at Jensyn and said that she was too pale and sickly for him to treat her, so we were sent back to the ED in Monticello. By the time we got her there, they did not feel qualified to deal with her, and, once again, she was ambulanced back to Children's, this time in Minneapolis—her home away from home.

By the time we joined her there, she had been admitted with an IV in her head so that they could get blood for tests and cultures. After receiving the test results, and once we knew that her white blood cell count was high, it was determined that she had a UTI, a kidney infection, and a blood infection. This all caused upper respiratory congestion, and to top it off, she had pink eye. That morning, we were told she was too sick for surgery and that it was the first canceled surgery in five years—maybe those red flags should have been further investigated right away when they saw them because, at this point, we had a very sick little girl.

This hospital stay ended up being long because she needed to be on ten days of IV antibiotics to fight the E. coli infection in her blood, but the bright spot was that she eventually got healthy enough to have her button surgery. We were thrilled that we would no longer have to be so careful with the long tubing that had caused so many issues. While they were doing the surgery, they attempted to put in a PICC (peripherally inserted central catheter) line so that we could have easier access to her blood and be able to administer her meds at home. A PICC line is used to deliver medications and other treatments directly into the large central veins near the heart and is often recommended for those who require frequent needle sticks for medicine or blood draws.

Once her button surgery was done, a different doctor was scheduled to put in the PICC line. After attempting for two hours, this doctor determined that her anatomy was such that he was unable to place it at this time. Jensyn became known for her extremely tiny and wonky veins. It was always a celebration when someone could properly draw blood or put in an IV. More unfortunate than the failed PICC line attempt was that she needed to stay in the hospital another five days to finish her course of IV meds. What's five more days away from home? It was starting to become our norm.

Feeding issues. Growth issues. Upper respiratory issues. Jensyn had been experiencing all of these issues from birth. At four months, she began to have seizures and UTIs. When something new came up regarding Jensyn's health, we were not really surprised anymore. Both Chris and I held an unspoken belief that, much like Britlyn's developmental delay, we would be able to figure out Jensyn's struggles with the proper interventions, medications, and therapies, and that she would get stronger and would eventually thrive. Hospital stays like this felt defeating. Everyone was doing all they could to keep her healthy and stay ahead of her needs, yet no matter what was done, nobody was able to do so.

The next few months of her first year of life continued to be plagued by illness and inpatient days in the hospital. More UTIs, more seizure issues, more gastrointestinal problems. We also began meeting with more specialists: we added an immunologist, a urologist, and a nephrologist to her team, and she had follow-up appointments with her pulmonologist and her cardiologist. We discovered that the small hole in her heart at birth had, in fact, closed up. It was wonderful to hear the cardiologist say that we could cross his name off our list of medical professionals since he claimed everything else with her heart looked good. In addition to these specialists, Jensyn also scored herself a helmet at this time in her journey. Because she spent so much time lying in hospital beds and favored one side of her sweet little head more than the other, her head was significantly flat on one side. Nobody could have looked cuter in a little pink helmet than Jensyn did. Of course, I had to be a little extra and add a large white bow to jazz it up.

Every week we were not at the hospital we were going to appointments, and in-home therapy had begun. I will never forget the day I ran errands alone in St. Cloud and called Britlyn's Birth to Three therapists. I remember struggling to articulate that Britlyn was doing great but that we needed their services once again and that I had given birth to another child with even more needs than Britlyn. It should have been a comfort to know this group of therapists already, and in some ways, it was. But it was also a vivid reminder that we were starting over and that people would once again regularly come into our home to work with another of our daughters.

The funny thing about being in the middle of a tricky and unpredictable situation is that many times it is difficult to see the reality as things unfold. As I said, Chris and I were convinced that Jensyn had just had a rough start to life and that we could get her past it to where she would eventually live a more normal life. Britlyn's issues, aside from her vision, were not medical in nature. We never worried that she would stop breathing or have a seizure or need any type of medical attention. And because I was not yet familiar with being a mom to a medically fragile child—we did not even classify her as such at this point—I will never forget the day her GI doctor rocked my world.

We were at a follow-up appointment to assess things with Jensyn's button. Early on, we decided I would always have someone with me when I went to appointments or took Jensyn anywhere since we never knew what could happen. Brinkley was my helper for this trip to meet with

Jensyn's gastroenterologist. We chatted with the nurse, who asked what was wrong with Jensyn. This question never bothered me, and I was happy to share what caused her to struggle and bring awareness to her rare condition. But then the doctor came in. I had not seen this doctor since her original GJ tube placement, so there had never been another chance for us to talk. He, too, asked me what caused Jensyn to be so sick. After I answered his question, he said, "How long is she supposed to live?"

I was shocked that he would ask this. And then I got mad. Chalk it up to being emotionally spent, but I was not interested in answering this question. I pointed at Brinkley and

"HOW LONG IS SHE SUPPOSED TO LIVE?"

said, "I don't know. How long is *she* supposed to live?" I was so angry somebody had the audacity to ask me such an insensitive question, but in hindsight, I think my reaction had more to do with the idea that Jensyn not living long had NEVER crossed my mind. Never! This was the first time I had been exposed to someone in the medical community who talked about death when I had wrongly assumed they were more concerned with life. Admittedly, this doctor probably did not mean to imply that he did not value life, but at that time, in the state of mind that I was in, my heart began to break because someone had planted the seed that Jensyn was more critical, more medically fragile than I had ever believed. I knew I was about to lose my grip on any control I had over this situation. It had become too big for me to handle, and I had zero idea what to do. The thought of ever actually losing a child was just not an option. It absolutely could not happen.

BROKEN

Throughout Jensyn's first six months of life, she had been in and out of the hospital so frequently that it had become difficult for me to fully understand the life I was trying to live. Of course, our family was super supportive. My parents and my in-laws were always available to stay with the kids so Chris and I could both be at the hospital, or they would be at the house so I could be with Jensyn while Chris continued to work. Neither of us wanted to take a break from our responsibilities or jobs, even though our commitments were strained at times.

The church was beyond supportive and told Chris he could focus on his family. He was able to be with me at the hospital whenever I needed him, and others were willing to cover any ministry needs he had. Our church family was overly generous with gas cards and gift cards for Chris and me to use on our many trips to the hospital or to appointments in the Twin Cities. Many, many people provided meals for the family when I could not be home. There were others who embraced our older kids and were willing to have them over or take them out to do fun things. As much as we appreciated this generosity, it was hard for me to accept it at times. It was a humbling lesson in allowing others to bless and care for my family. It was hard, but it was also beautiful; I will never forget it.

I will always remember one particular act of service. I was sitting on the couch in the NICU when I received a reply to a message I had sent to my friend Beth. Beth was a reading teacher at the public school, and I had simply asked her if she knew anyone who could help teach my Brinkley to read. My first four kids did not struggle with reading, and Brinkley, who was almost eight, was finding it difficult to grasp. I had planned to focus on reading that year in school, and not being able to do so was one more thing that kept me awake at night. I so badly wanted Brinkley to find success in this area, and it felt like we were losing time, with me always at the hospital. Instead of giving me a reference for someone who might be able to help, Beth said that she would do it herself. She said that if she could take one thing off my plate, teaching Brinkley to read was something she knew how to do. This act of love for me and for my daughter meant so much to me. It was one of many times that someone's generosity left me in tears while I sat in the hospital, feeling helpless.

Friends were also super integral in my ability to keep my head above water during this time. I remember one friend asking me what I needed most, to which

MY LIFE HAD VIRTUALLY SHUT DOWN, YET THEY WERE STILL LIVING THEIRS.

I replied, "I need to do something with my friends that I would normally do." Going out for supper or coffee and talking all night felt like something that would make the ambivalence of my days feel more settled. So my friends did this for me. They made dinner plans and took me out for coffee. If I was at the hospital, they would come to see me. But strangely, as much as all those moments meant to me and as much as I loved catching up with each of them and hearing about their lives, it left me feeling weirdly alone and detached. Those visits mostly served as a reminder of what they were doing and what I was unable to do. My life had virtually shut down, yet they were still living theirs.

Naturally, as a Christian, I should have been able to snap out of the funk I was in. At least, that is what I had always believed. If I shared my concerns with friends, some would ask me about my time in the Word or if I was praying about my struggles. Obviously, I knew I should have been doing those things. Ironically, I've noticed that when I have been at my lowest points in life, turning to

God has often been difficult for me. This new feeling of spiritual paralysis took me back to the time when we lost our first baby, and my pastor's wife said that when we are going through tough things, it is okay to let others do the praying for us. That memory comforted me, but I still could not wrap my brain around what to do to make me feel more like myself again.

Sometimes, other family members would stay with Jensyn so that I could go to church. But it felt like "church" had moved on without me. Even in a public setting such as that, I felt disconnected and distant, like I was in a different world, living a divergent life. My brain could not focus on anything most of the time as it was always trying to stay one step ahead of the next big thing that was sure to happen with Jensyn. It was no way to live.

One night in April 2017, I was working out at the gym by our house, and while I was on the treadmill, I was listening to worship music, which had become my go-to during this time of my spiritual drought. Singing praise is what helped me feel connected to the Lord. I also found myself crying out to God about what to do. What could I do to fix these feelings of despair that I was having? As a believer, there seems to be a certain idea about how one should act in difficult situations, and I also had the unique challenge of being a pastor's wife. Even though nobody ever voiced how they expected me to handle the tough stuff, I still felt like I needed to set an example. I just did not have the resolve to set one. I was a hot mess.

So, I cried out to the Lord, and every time I did, He would gently bring a person's name to mind. This person had not been at our church for as long as I had been, and she did not really know me. I believe God connected us because of this, though. Here is what I texted her after leaving the gym in tears that night:

April 3, 2017

Hi Marcia,

I am sure it is no secret that life has not gone according to my plan these past seven months. I have loved Jesus my entire life and would tell anyone else in my position to press into God. Those words don't mean anything when I have not previously been where I am now. See, I know what to do and I cannot do it. For the life of me, I cannot press into God, no matter how hard I try. My prayer life is nothing, and my devotional life is the driest it has ever been. I am broken and I do not know how to do broken.

So why am I telling you all of this? I have no idea, other than every time I cry out to God about what I am supposed to do to figure out this new life, your name comes to mind. Every. Single. Time. So, I am just reaching out. Maybe just to get some prayer. Maybe to get some fresh ideas. Mostly just trying to be obedient

to God. So, do with this as you feel led. Thank you for
being an example of someone worthy of reaching out
to!

Blessings,
Kristin

Almost immediately, Marcia replied. "Dear Kristin,
Thank you for reaching out. I am wondering if you would
like to meet."

We met a couple of days later. She helped me figure
out my feelings, asked if I thought I might be dealing with
postpartum depression, and suggested that I embrace
being broken while giving those jagged pieces to the Lord
in my own timing and in a way that made sense to me.
Never did she question why I was not praying or spending
time in the Word. She allowed me to live deep in my
reality and gave me the grace to eventually claw my way
out. And she was with me through it all.

Full disclosure: I did decide to consult a doctor
about the possibility of postpartum depression. With
seven other babies, I had never struggled with anything
more than a short stint with the baby blues, yet this
was obviously nothing like my other postpartum days.
There was no time to recover from Jensyn's birth. My
body had been in fight-or-flight mode since the moment
she entered this world, and it became clear that I just

might need a little help to quiet the dissonance that was happening in my brain because of it.

I saw a doctor I had never seen before because I was able to piggyback my appointment with one of Jensyn's later that week. As we discussed how I was feeling, this doctor agreed that perhaps trying a medication might be what I needed to regulate things. So, for the first time ever, I took what I called "my crazy pills." It took several weeks for them to take effect, and although I felt less scattered, I also felt less alive. I did not love how I felt, or lack of "felt," on the meds, but I wanted to give them a fair chance.

This experience with depression and medication opened my eyes to another area of empathy I had grossly misunderstood. Previously, I had been in the camp that believed a person who was depressed should be able to snap out of it—mind over matter, take your thoughts captive, give it to Jesus, pray—but I soon learned that when someone is going through it, it is nearly impossible to regain control over your emotions. For me, I needed a reset. With that came a deep understanding and remorse for those who deal with depression on the daily. I never want to be there again.

Marcia continued to meet with me, and her mentorship turned into a deep friendship that remains to this day. She shared her life struggles with me as I shared mine with her, and she became such a pillar of strength in my journey with Jensyn. Her commitment to my family and to my walk with Jesus has meant everything to me, and I will forever be grateful that the Lord encouraged me to reach out to her during a low point in my life and that she was willing to reach down and help lift me out of my despair.

I mentioned in my initial text to Marcia that I was broken and that I did not know how to do broken. Grasping this concept was something else God was teaching me through Jensyn. At one point, when I was sitting in the hospital, holding my girl, I had just finished reading *The Broken Way* by Ann Voskamp. She wrote, "When we live broken, we have something to give to others. When we live in the FEAR of being broken, trying to be perfect, we have nothing of value to give." Unintentionally, I am pretty sure that I had lived in fear of ever being broken. And now that there were big, huge pieces of broken in my life, I was beginning to see that my daughter and the rest of my family did not need me to be perfect. If anyone was broken in the world's eyes, it was my sweet Jensyn, who had been fighting for her life since the day she was born. Yet, in my eyes, there was nothing more perfect than this child I had been given. I was starting to see that perhaps I was more broken than she. And *this* is exactly where God needed me to be.

HOPE IN THE HARD

I t is never easy for a parent to watch one of their children struggle to live. Yet, as hard as it was for me and as concerned as I was about Jensyn, not being able to be a full-time mom to my other kids was an entirely different kind of difficult. That first year was a blur for all of us as we did what we could to figure out how life with Jensyn would be. I believe we all thought her health would eventually level out and we would have the chance to collectively care for her at home, just as it had happened with Britlyn. However, we gradually realized that we had no clue how this life was going to pan out, so we rallied together and made things work the best we knew how.

When Jensyn was nine months old, Max graduated from Cornerstone Academy Homeschool. It was bizarre to think that I was graduating my firstborn while still having a baby at home. I recall a photo of Max in his cap and gown, proudly holding his baby sister. Blessedly, Jensyn was healthy at this time, and because Max's graduation was in May, we felt it was safe enough to begin taking Jensyn out in public a little bit more. Max's ceremony and party were a huge success, and I thoroughly enjoyed using the creative planning side of my brain to throw him a big celebration.

That summer, Jensyn continued to be in and out of the hospital, but we managed to find some time to make memories as a family. By the end of the summer, however, two huge transitions happened in our lives, and preparing for them took anything extra we had to give.

Max would soon leave home for college—he had been accepted at the University of Northwestern, formerly Northwestern College, of which Chris and I were proud alums. Even with his planned move-out, we were at the point where our home was no longer a good fit for our family. It had never crossed our minds to move, but with his impending departure and the growing need for space as our children got older, we realized we had to make some changes. It seemed more than crazy to move during this tumultuous time in our lives, but when our friend shared that she knew of a home for sale that would be perfect for us, we agreed and snatched it up. We spent most of our free days in the summer boxing up thirteen years of life. Since moving to Becker in 2004, we had lived in the same twin home—four bedrooms and three bathrooms for ten people. Although we have always believed it is good for siblings to share rooms, the general living spaces no longer accommodated our needs.

With her many therapies and needs, Jensyn was acquiring more and more equipment and machines. It was getting increasingly difficult for her in-home therapists to have enough space to work with her. Jensyn was also still sleeping in our room, which we knew was not a long-term option for any of us. She needed her own space, and we longed to be able to spread out. The house we purchased had five bedrooms and an office that could be used as a bedroom if needed. Most of the kids would still share a room, but getting Jensyn more space was our priority. Brinkley offered to bunk in with her, and we eventually took her up on her offer.

Moving with eight kids is hard enough, but moving while still juggling appointments and hospital stays and getting a kid ready for college was next-level craziness. Of course, on top of packing up the old house, there was painting and prepping to do at the new house to add a personal touch before we moved in. All of this was a welcome distraction from the life we were living, yet saying goodbye to the walls that held thirteen years of memories proved to be more emotional than I thought it would be. Max left for college in August, and we left our home on River Street in September. Emotions were high, but we were excited to be in our new house, and it proved to be a good move for all of us.

Fall came shortly after our move, and that meant I would soon be keeping Jensyn home again amid the cold and flu season. Fortunately, we were still able to take her to church in October for her dedication service. Although she clearly had a strong connection to the Lord and had already been prayed for by so many people, we wanted to publicly give her back to God and recognize that He loves her more than we ever could. We made our commitment to raise her, to provide for her, and to teach her about Jesus—something we felt very privileged to be able to do. To sweeten the day, Tygen chose to declare his commitment to Jesus publicly, so we also got to celebrate his baptism later that same day.

Traveling with Jensyn was difficult and risky, but we had not been to South Dakota to see my parents since she was born. She seemed pretty strong around Thanksgiving, so we decided to give it a go. We did not plan to stay very long and felt the risk was worth going. My brother, Jeff, and his family were also going to be there, so it would be fun for the cousins to see each other. Because my parents' house was not large enough to accommodate all of us, they rented a few hotel rooms. Rather than hauling Jensyn back and forth, we arranged to have her stay at the house with Maci, who would tend to any needs that might arise.

Chris and I stayed at the hotel with the other girls while the boys also stayed at Grandma and Grandpa's house.

We enjoyed the time together, and my brother, who loves babies, was getting lots of Jensyn cuddles. All went well that first night, but on Thanksgiving, Jensyn seemed to be getting a bit of a cold again. Chris and I were confident that Maci and my mom could care for Jensyn, so we took the three girls back to the hotel for the evening after all the festivities. By the time we had driven to the hotel, Maci had already called once to say that she had witnessed several seizures and thought we should know. And then, at 1:30 a.m., she called to say that Jensyn's feeding tube button had popped out. This was not the first time this had happened to her button, so we knew it could happen rather easily. In fact, just a few weeks prior, I had pulled it out while trying to pick her up. The button popping out is not an emergency, but how quickly the hole in her tummy can close up is.

We told Maci to call 911, and we called my sister-in-law Lori to come stay in our room at the hotel with the girls. By the time we got to the house, the EMTs were there, but they had absolutely no idea what to do with Jensyn. Chris and I asked them for medical tape, and we taped the button the best we could and rode with the ambulance to the hospital. Once we got there, they still did not know what to do with a baby with such complicated needs. We attempted to tell the nurses that a GJ tube needed to be placed by a radiologist, so they checked to see if one was on call. We were told we would have to wait until the next morning for a radiologist to do it. Meanwhile, the ED doctor finally came in; he picked up the old button, washed it in the sink, and shoved it back into Jensyn's tummy. Without a word to Chris or me, he walked out. After such a bizarre experience and knowing what we knew about how these buttons typically get replaced, we knew that we needed to get Jensyn back to Children's, where they would know how to best take care of her. So, that is what we did.

We borrowed my parents' car and left Aberdeen at 3:51 a.m. to drive straight to Children's. When we got to the ED, Jensyn was having seizures and was pretty congested. We had not been giving her any food because we believed the tube was not in the correct position. The ED nurse took one look at Jensyn and got her in right away. Once we got to radiology, the radiologist decided he would need to do an X-ray to see where exactly the Aberdeen doctor had shoved the feeding tube. He was dumbfounded—in twenty-one years of practice, this doctor had never seen a GJ tube shoved into place without the help of radiology.

Perhaps we bolted too quickly and should have just waited to see radiology in the morning back in Aberdeen, but we had learned that when Jensyn gets sick, she gets sick quickly, and we need to be close to good care when it happens. My mom drove our fifteen-passenger van back with the rest of the family the next day. Although we had been able to celebrate Thanksgiving with my family, this was the last time Jensyn ever visited Aberdeen, and it was becoming more apparent that holiday celebrations would best be had at home.

Jensyn was born toward the end of 2016, and her life in 2017 was anything but easy. It was a doozy of a year for all of us, so perhaps some of the thoughts I shared in our Christmas letter for that year best recap our emotions around how we weathered the crazy:

For us, this past year was all about a new reality for our family, and we are doing our best to figure out how to live in that reality. Every time I thought about what I should share for 2017, one word kept coming to mind: HARD! And much like I don't want to keep doing hard, I haven't really wanted to write about it either. However, our life is hard right now, and to sugarcoat our year just wouldn't be accurate.

Hard—There are many different definitions of this word, but the one that applies to the hard I am talking about is: "requiring a great deal of endurance or effort." Yep—that kind of hard!

Hard—Max went to college this fall. Saying goodbye to him and leaving him at this new "home" was one of the hardest things we have ever had to do as parents. To be so excited for his future and so sad about his being out of the house at the same time is an emotion that cannot fully be explained. Obviously, it has changed the dynamics of our home, and it has been HARD!

Hard—As if we didn't have enough going on in our lives, we realized that the Lord was allowing us the opportunity to move into a home that better fit the size of our family. We've accepted this gift for what it is, but leaving a home that we absolutely loved for 13 years and navigating a move in the midst of school starting and Chris' busiest time of the year in youth ministry required an insane amount of emotional and physical strength. It was unbelievably HARD!

Hard—Being a homeschool family whose biggest desire is to school our children at home and give them every opportunity we can, it was not an easy decision to send Britlyn to public school once again. We have always said that we would do whatever is in the best interest of our kids, but sending one child away each day, even if it is the best choice for her, is HARD!

Hard—Having a baby experience 15 ED visits, 8 ambulance rides, and 12 hospital stays, which equaled 61 total days in the hospital, is hard! At 15 months, Jensyn is still an enigma to the doctors who work

*with her. She has multiple seizures every day, and
we cannot find the meds to help her get relief. She is
100% tube-fed and has begun feeding therapy to keep
her mouth interested in possibly eating someday. She
does PT and OT every week in our home and has just
qualified for a significant amount of PCA hours for
the coming year. She has not smiled or responded to
us since early summer, which we believe is due to the
seizures. She was just fitted for a medical stroller, which
looks an awful lot like a wheelchair. Seeing her struggle
and doing all that we can to meet her every need, often
at the expense of time with the rest of the family, is
HARD!*

*Hard—I think we always assumed we knew what
it meant for life to be hard, but never have we
experienced hard like this. There have been days when
life is just too much, moments when we just cannot
make sense of anything that is going on, opportunities
that are not possible because we cannot handle one
more thing. When I really stopped to think about this
word, I had to ask myself what the opposite of hard
is. But then, I thought about it a bit differently, and
it is at times such as these that I am so grateful for
a God who cares enough to give us the answer. The
obvious opposite of hard is easy, but we have never
been promised easy. Easy will never be our reality on*

this side of heaven. However, at the end of hard, there is always HOPE! Actually, hope does not just come at the end of hard; Hope has always been. Hope exists IN the hard, and Hope comes BEFORE the hard. God sent Jesus as our HOPE to help with our HARD. As hard as this past year has been, there has been so much hope. Sometimes, it has been hard to see that hope in the dailiness of life, but it is crystal clear in the reflection.

Hope—Max went to college this fall. He is thriving and loving every aspect of his experience there. He is close enough to home that we see him often. Knowing that he is doing well offers so much HOPE!

Hope—We never anticipated moving, but the orchestration of it all was the Lord's doing. The sellers of our new home graciously accepted our offer, and after just two showings of our old home, we received our full asking price. Our church family and friends pitched in wholeheartedly to help us move and set up our new place. Not a day goes by that we don't feel utterly blessed to be living in this house, and we are excited about what the future holds for us here. This is HOPE!

Hope—Having the privilege to homeschool our kids for the past 12 years is such a blessing. In a perfect world, they would all be home learning from us, but for Britlyn, public school is exactly what she needs. She is reading and figuring out stuff that I would have never thought to challenge her to learn. The foundation that is being laid for her education and for her life skills will hopefully be enough that we can someday bring her home to learn with us. That is our HOPE!

Hope—Obviously, if we could change the trajectory of Jensyn's future to be one with fewer struggles, we would do whatever is asked of us. And this is true for our entire family. To see how the kids have stepped up to help with Jensyn, to look after each other when Jensyn has appointments or is sick, or to take over for Chris or me when we need a break from it all has been such a gift. The joy that this sweet girl has brought our family as we continue to figure out life with her offers an unbelievable amount of HOPE!

If we truly did get to author our own stories, I wonder how differently we would write them. I would like to say that I would choose to include the hard, but if I am completely honest, I would rather have easy. However, there is no growth in easy. There is no depth of emotion or change of heart in easy. There is no need for others to do life with us in easy. And above all, there is no need for a Savior in easy!

As hard as 2017 has been for our family, there is absolutely no doubt that we have been stretched to grow in ways we never thought possible. The emotional and heart-wrenching moments have brought us to the end of ourselves over and over again. Needing the body of Christ to pray when we haven't had words or to hold us up when we were just too weary to even know what to do next has been humbling. And, we have always known about our need for Jesus, but this year we have NEEDED Jesus. I guess it is a good thing that we aren't the ones penning how our lives will live out. Without the hard, where is the hope? We have learned that when we focus on the HARD, we lose sight of the HOPE. It is our goal to focus on the HOPE that still rescues the HARD!

Obviously, even in the hoping, the hard did not cease to exist. In fact, even with interventions and therapies and all the things, Jensyn continued to struggle. Somehow, we made it through life with our little girl for a year and a half, and as we hoped for an easier year ahead, we knew that no matter what, God could be trusted.

PROVISION AND THE PICU

Although some things that were part of Britlyn's story are also part of Jensyn's, there was so much more to be learned the second time around. Once we joined Birth to Three with Britlyn, she received a case manager from the county. This person was vital in helping us figure out services, grants, and funds available when caring for a child with special needs. When Britlyn was three, she qualified for a grant to get her own iPad, which ironically helped her learn some speech. "Talking Tom" was an app she used daily, and she was soon able to mimic what this quirky cat said. She also qualified to get other things she needed for her development: special shoe inserts, manipulative books and toys, and other things.

Each year, the county reassesses each child's needs and decides what would best suit them for the upcoming year. When Brilyn was about to turn five, we had our final meeting with Christine, her outstanding case manager from the county. Britlyn was doing so well at this point she no longer qualified for any services. It was thrilling for her to "graduate" from the program.

Now, it was Jensyn's turn. Again, I called Christine, and again, a friend from Britlyn's team joined Jensyn's team. It became clear that Jensyn's needs were far more significant than Britlyn's ever had been, so in January 2018, we began adding paid staff to our story. The first person we hired was Max's girlfriend, Sidney. She was going to school to be an occupational therapy assistant and was perfect for the job of caring for our little girl. She agreed to work with Jensyn as needed each week. Maci also joined the payroll as she continued to offer loving care for her sister.

Initially, Sidney came when we wanted to go somewhere as a family but needed to keep Jensyn home. For example, for Tate's eleventh birthday, she stayed with Jensyn while the rest of us went to a movie. It was refreshing to have someone available to help with Jensyn's rising needs so that we could go out and do something together. We had known Sidney and her family for many years—she and Max

HAVING OTHERS COME INTO THE HOME TO HELP US WITH JENSYN'S CARE WAS SUCH A GIFT.

had actually gone to kindergarten together, but both were homeschooled later on. Sidney is also the oldest of eight kids, so our hectic home did not intimidate her, and having her around so much made it easier for us to get to know her better as well. Of course, since Max wanted Sidney to come with us sometimes, we hired another PCA (personal care assistant) for such moments. Laura worked with Jensyn for several years and loved spending time with the other girls as well. Having Laura come "work" for the day was always a treat. Her great love for Jensyn blessed us all, and we could trust that Jensyn was loved and cared for when we were away.

Having others come into the home to help us with Jensyn's care was such a gift. Maci already knew how to work the feeding pump and administer the great number of meds that we had to pump through the feeding tube, but soon, Sidney was trained to give meds and monitor feeds as well. This was no small thing as we gave meds three times daily and refilled the milk bag every few hours. Another person helping allowed for fewer interruptions to our homeschooling days. It was a true blessing.

Sidney would often try to time her hours to coincide with the therapists' visits. With her training in OT, she was also fascinated by the physical therapy and other treatments Jensyn had. Learning all she could, Sidney was instrumental in helping us work with Jensyn to strengthen her core, stretch out her low-toned arms and legs, and help her progress with her head control. Macrocephaly (medical term for a large melon) was becoming a more prominent problem for Jensyn; her large head was often too much for her to hold up on her own. Sidney would often join me for Jensyn's appointments as well. Together, we learned so much about how best to care for Jensyn and enjoyed working together on her behalf.

Because of this help and because Jensyn was getting a little stronger in her second year of life, we found we were not running to the hospital quite as often as we were the first year. However, we still had to watch her very closely when she got sick. We already knew that when Jensyn tanked, she tanked fast and needed to be under medical supervision quickly.

Back when we were trying to figure out why Jensyn kept getting so sick during the first year of her life, our hospital stays would be brief—a few days here and there to get some answers and sometimes a week to fully recover. Yet, as she got older, her bouts of sickness got worse, and our first extended, scary hospital stay happened in March 2018.

Jensyn was supposed to have had a procedure done to check her hearing and to do an esophageal scope since we were still working on her swallow. However, like what happened when she was supposed to get her GJ tube button placed, she spiked a fever and got a cold the night before. Perhaps Jenysn was trying to tell us she was not interested in these surgeries and procedures! This time, we did not bother to take her in; we just rescheduled the surgery. As that day wore on, Jensyn got sicker and sicker, so we decided to tap out and call for someone more qualified to take over. By this time, we'd learned that calling the ambulance always trumped the decision to drive her ourselves. Fortunately, one of us was always able to accompany her to the hospital so we could help care for her and advocate for her needs.

When we arrived at the hospital, Jensyn's breathing was definitely getting more labored. They did blood work, and Jensyn tested positive for RSV (respiratory syncytial virus), one of the horrible viruses that we had tried so hard to shield her from. Unfortunately, when you live in a home with as many people as we have, it is nearly impossible to keep everyone healthy all the time. Many of the other kids at home were currently sick with the flu and other bugs. Jensyn did not stand a chance of avoiding illness, no matter how hard we tried.

This virus was a nasty one. The doctors told us that days three through five are usually when this virus peaks and actually gets worse before it gets better. We were on a regular floor at Children's in Minneapolis. Both Children's Hospitals in Minnesota are teaching hospitals, which means that medical students and residents work as a team to tend to the patients on the regular floors. A doctor oversees each team and helps guide their decisions. Ultimately, the rounding doctor can make any final decisions that are necessary. My teacher's heart had always been open to students working with Jensyn, especially considering how she offered a complex situation for them to learn about. Sometimes, it was confusing to know who was calling the shots, but we had never encountered any significant issues . . . until this stay.

We had been at the hospital for four days, and Jensyn was doing precisely what the doctors said she would do: she had gotten worse on day three and struggled even more on day four. Her oxygen needs had increased, and they were suctioning secretions around the clock. Of all the respiratory issues she had experienced, this was the worst she had ever been. At one point that morning, some friends stopped by to see us. We looked in the crib at Jensyn, who was listless and weak. Her labored breathing was hard to watch. Shortly after our visitors left, I went to the cafeteria to grab lunch. Jensyn's struggle was heavy on my mind.

When I returned upstairs to head back to our room, I saw Jensyn's pulmonologist working at a desk at the end of the hall. It felt like an answer to prayer. Immediately, I asked her if she was here to see Jensyn, to which she replied, "I did not know Jensyn was here." What?! Before I could even register my confusion, I shared that she was not doing well and that I wanted her to give an opinion.

When she told me she would have to ask the resident on Jensyn's team before she could do that, I realized then that hospital protocol is a thing. I also decided that I did not like it.

Once she was given the "okay" to come see *her* patient, things switched into high gear. Jensyn's pulmonologist examined her, quickly changed her meds and respiratory therapies, and called the rounding physician. Within minutes, she had Jensyn transferred to the PICU (Pediatric Intensive Care Unit). Although I was grateful for this necessary intervention, it was suddenly so much to absorb. I knew Jensyn was sick, but sick enough for a unit like that?

Aside from the NICU, we had never been on such a critical floor. It felt like being in a fishbowl: all glass doors, one-on-one nurses, a couch, but no shower. I had no idea how life worked for me when my daughter was a patient in the PICU, but I was about to find out. There are no medical students on this floor. All the doctors are intensivists, and all nurses are highly skilled in this type of care. I got a chance to talk to the resident who was heading up Jensyn's team on the regular floor before we were officially transferred. I asked him why the pulmonologist had not been alerted to our presence in the hospital.

"Because you never told me she was followed by pulmonology," he said.

I asked if he had bothered to check her chart, but his nonresponse was response enough. So many times, we could see God's fingerprints on Jensyn's life, and we had witnessed some pretty amazing things since the day she was born. This was another example of Him compensating for an oversight and rescuing Jensyn from human error as well as from my unknown negligence in divulging her list of doctors.

Obviously, this was a learning experience for me. Never again would I hold back information, even inadvertently. Never again would I assume that anybody working with Jensyn knew anything. And I would always be the one to advocate for whatever Jensyn needed. Typically, I don't have Mama Bear tendencies, but when it came to getting the absolute best care for my child, there were moments where a little bit of bear eked out. For that I would never apologize because I would always do whatever it took for Jensyn.

Jensyn was in the PICU for seven days after being on the regular floor for four. After being in the step-down unit for three more days, we were able to go home. Fourteen days in the hospital—it was our longest stay so far. Although Chris and I traded off one night at the beginning of this stay, I was with Jensyn for most of the rest of those two weeks. Hospital stays had become common for our family, but long stays were new. We had no way of knowing that some of our future stays would be far longer than this!

BLURRY SNAPSHOTS

Hospital stays were taxing; the entire family felt the tension of their frequency. Even though the kids said they understood why I had to be with Jensyn, I often found myself trying to process how they were handling everything. There was plenty of time to wonder and worry as I sat in the hospital apart from them.

I wondered how they felt in those early days when they witnessed Jensyn not eating well and turning blue. What went through their minds when Chris and I raced out of the house to drive their sister to the emergency room? How did they feel about how often we called 911? When they were not home and heard an ambulance, did it affect them? Did they assume it was heading for Jensyn? What was it like to be going about their lives at home when suddenly, there would be first responders, policemen, firemen, and EMTs clustered in the house, ready to load up their sister to take her back to the hospital? And what about when I suddenly had to drop everything to quickly pack a bag so I could ride along in the ambulance?

Of course, we talked about it. From the very first time Jensyn was sick, we shared with the kids how severe things were, and we made sure to tell them when things were getting better as well. The lines of communication were always open for them to ask questions, and any chance we could, we gave them the opportunity to go to the hospital to see their sister and me. Often, when they witnessed Jensyn on oxygen and saw the other tubes pumping life into their frail sister, they better understood why I was unable to be home.

> IT WAS THEN THAT I SAW A REALITY THAT WAS NOT NORMAL TO OTHERS BUT, SADLY, HAD BECOME NORMAL TO US.

It was the summer after we moved into our new house. I have no idea how many times we had called 911 prior to this day, but what transpired next opened my eyes in a way I have never forgotten. Jensyn's pulse-ox registered numbers in the 80s, which was far too low. She was sleepy and listless, yet we chose to wait and see what would happen.

As we fed the kids lunch and made phone calls to nurses, Chris and I knew we were prolonging the inevitable. Holding Jensyn in my arms, trying to wake her up, led to a seizure, so we called 911—again.

The kids knew something was up, as they always did. I would like to say everything moved quickly at this point— and in some ways, it did— but the blurry pictures I saw from the outside looking in were a slow-motion rendering. When I got to the hospital that night, I began to replay the day in my mind. I saw fuzzy pictures, like something you see in a dream when looking down at life around you. As I reflected, it was then I saw a reality that was not normal to others but, sadly, had become normal to us.

I saw these snapshots:

The first responders standing at our back door.

Two policemen starting Jensyn on oxygen.

Three firemen joining the policemen as we told our story over and over as they documented our daughter's issues.

Me—texting a friend to take Tygen to basketball. She didn't even ask why. She just handled it. The same friend came over and offered to take Britlyn and Jakely to her house. They went willingly.

The EMTs coming to assess the situation. Our home was once again packed with too many adults hovering over our little girl. They loaded Jensyn up to take her in.

Sidney showing up because I had forgotten to tell her Jensyn would not need her that day. She helped me pack my bag. We looked for Jensyn's sweet llama named Lucy. We needed Lucy, and we found her.

Me—walking out to the ambulance to accompany my daughter to Children's.

Brinkley—outside at a friend's house. She asked me for a hug goodbye, no tears, and returned to playing with her friend.

Me—giving Tate a quick squeeze. He showed no emotion, just a resigned look of understanding.

Me—in the ambulance, doing what I always did, emotionless. I grabbed my phone and took the same picture I have taken so many other times: my daughter, asleep, with an oxygen mask covering most of her face.

Me—conversing with the EMT and answering all of her questions.

Me—texting our friends and family, asking them to pray, sending the picture I had just taken in the ambulance, the one I always send.

Me—texting my children, Maci at work to let her know that the ambulance was once again in our neighborhood and that it was there for Jensyn. She texted back a thumbs up. And Max, to let him know we were heading to the hospital. He replied, "I know. Somebody already told me."

When Jensyn was first sick, I would have seen different pictures. There used to be tears. There used to be clingy hugs and emotions that were all over the place. I was glad our kids knew and believed that Chris and I were doing everything we could to care for their sister, yet it broke my heart to think this had become common for them—that they would willingly go with friends, a quick hug or a squeeze goodbye sufficed, and a heads-up text was all they needed. This tugged at me in a way that I could not even describe. Maybe they knew that Jensyn was not as sick this time as she had been other times, but probably they were just so used to this being our reality.

I never doubted their love for their sister, and I knew that with everything in them, they hated that she got sick so often. I knew they believed God was in control. Maybe this was just how they had to cope while waiting for God to make things a little less fuzzy for all of us, but these images of my children, the vague responses to my texts, the reticent understanding of this life that we were living was hard to bear. And for a mom who likes to fix what is broken, I did not know the remedy for this.

Even more difficult for me to comprehend was the battle Chris fought as the parent who stayed behind. There is no doubt he felt torn each time, wanting to support Jensyn and me but also knowing that someone needed to meet the needs of the other kids. Perhaps the kids cried after I left. I know there were questions and concerns that he had to deal with on his own. Rarely did he worry me with any of it; he just handled it. As much as ambulance rides and hospital stays had become common in our kids' lives, how Chris and I approached them also had become common. I went. He stayed. Yet, even while separated, we were always united in the fight for our family. The kids knew that, and maybe that was enough.

MISDIAGNOSED

S ometimes, we had scheduled hospital stays, which were much easier to prepare for than emergent ones. In the summer of 2018, we were back in the hospital, but this time, it was our first planned stay. Seizures continued to plague Jensyn, and we had tried all kinds of medicines to combat them. Watching a child seize has to be one of the worst things in this world. Even worse than watching, though, is the helpless feeling, knowing that nothing can be done in the moment to stop them.

After months of trying to figure out her seizures and after trying several different med combinations, Jensyn's neurologist was humble enough to say he felt we should get a second opinion. He referred us to Dr. Smith with the Minnesota Epilepsy Group. When we first started meeting with Dr. Smith, he did an initial EEG to determine Jensyn's baseline seizure activity. He said that although he wasn't seeing a lot of active seizures, he was seeing an increase in Jensyn's background brain activity. This needed to be calmed down because if it continued the way it was, it would affect her development going forward.

Because of this information, Dr. Smith suggested we try switching Jensyn to the ketogenic diet, which fascinates me. He explained that when people had seizures "back in Bible times," it was believed that the person was possessed. Since the priests could not allow that, they would make the sick person fast. This caused the seizures to stop. The intent was to find a way to trick the body into fasting or into thinking it was fasting. That is what the keto diet does—it retrains the brain to think it is fasting. Some kids with seizures have found relief by following the ketogenic diet, so this seemed like a logical next step for us.

Transitioning a child to this diet takes a little finesse and a lot of observation, so they only do this inpatient. And since epilepsy patients and those with seizures are housed and treated most often at the Children's Hospital in St. Paul, that was where we went. This was our first stay at a place we would grow to love. At the time, we thought Minneapolis was our home away from home, but we would soon find out just how much the crew in St. Paul would make it feel even more like a home as they became like family to us.

Jensyn had great care during her diet switch, and we were only there for five days before they turned us loose to finish navigating the transition on our own. Being on the keto diet meant changing Jensyn's formula. Before the change, we could dump regular formula into her milk bag. Now, we had a specific recipe to follow that contained a ratio fashioned to her needs. We were followed by a dietician who helped us tweak her recipe as different needs presented themselves. Each morning, we had to measure and mix this formula, which she was still fed slowly, twenty-three hours a day.

Since keto eliminates carbohydrates, we also had to switch all of Jensyn's medications to pill form. Before, we had used liquid meds and were able to use syringes to inject them into a port in her feeding tube. It was easy and effective. Liquid meds, however, have added sugars and carbs, so we had to change how we administered her meds, too. We now had to crush up each pill, do what we could to dissolve them in water, and then use a syringe to suck up as much of this new solution as possible. It was a much more laborious process, which increased over time as new meds were added to her arsenal. Obviously, our goal was to keep her in a state of ketosis in an attempt to ward off the dreaded and damaging seizures. Although the transition to keto went well, we did not witness an immediate improvement. Regardless, we figured it could only help and decided to give it more time.

The transition continued to go well until Jensyn
got sick again. Just a month after being in the hospital
to transition her onto the diet, Jensyn began to struggle
with her oxygen and had a nasty seizure. The ambulance
picked her up; this time, we had them take us to St.
Paul Children's again. We were told that because the
epilepsy doctors now followed her, we should make this
our preferred hospital. Same story; different day. This
time, aspiration pneumonia and another UTI were the
suspected culprits of her quick decline.

After being there a day, she seemed to be getting
stronger and did not even need to be on oxygen. As
we waited for blood and urine cultures to return, we
accepted care from the doctors. After determining there
was no pneumonia or anything respiratory, the only
positive test we had was a confirmed UTI. They started a
med to fight that, and I was sure it would be a short stay.
Instead, Jensyn began to cry in pain like we had never
heard before, and seizures were not far behind. Because
of these changes, she needed oxygen.

Here we go again.

Her pained cries had become so consistent that, at
one point, Jensyn had to be given Ativan to help calm her
down. Ativan works to slow the activity of the brain and
nerves. It also can stop painful spasms in muscles and
sometimes prevent life-threatening seizures. It is often
a drug of last resort when nothing else offers comfort. I

hated that we had to give it to her, but I hated to hear her excruciating crying more. Not knowing what was causing the pain was disconcerting, and I knew that we could not go home without answers. So, I hunkered down to stay for as long as it would take to get them.

Three days into this hospital stay, Chris had plans to take Maci and several others in the youth group to Montana for Adventure Camp. He debated staying back, but we felt confident Jensyn would be fine, so he left with the youth, and my mom came to be with the kids at home. Not long after he had arrived in Montana, Jensyn began to struggle. Here is an excerpt from Jensyn's journal:

July 15, 2018

Well, we had another rough night last night! Around 9:00, you started crying again. You had been weepy all day, but I hoped you would just crash tonight. We tried for a while to figure out what might be wrong. Earlier in the day, they hooked you up to an EEG. While on this floor, techs watch the EEG around the clock. They began to notice that you were having cluster seizures. It was nauseating for me to watch. Your head would shake, and then your arms. Your eyes reminded me of those creepy baby dolls whose eyes just keep rolling and moving and never close. You seemed so miserable.

They decided to give you your rescue med like we use when you have seizures at home. We gave one dose and waited five minutes. It did nothing for you. We gave the second dose, and it still didn't seem to do much overall. Your oxygen dropped, so we upped that. Finally, you did settle down, and around 2:00 a.m., you fell asleep. They had a big drug on hand called phenobarbital. This drug is used in large quantities to put someone in a coma. I was glad we did not need to use it.

At 5:30 a.m., your nurse woke me to say that you were cluster seizing again. They had to give you the big drug. It is now 9:40 p.m., and you have not been awake all day. Ugh. Your sweet self must be so tired. The doctors were concerned today and said that you have thrown them off a bit. They said they felt the need to start over, so they redid your labs. The on-call neurologist came by as well. He said he thinks you are just having new seizures, and we need to rethink your current meds. I have been all over the place today. Freaked out a bit this morning. But I am hopeful you will be more awake tomorrow.

Dad had a rough day today as well. Yesterday, he left for Adventure Camp with Maci. He heard about your night—he actually called last night and heard you

*crying. He was ready to fly home to be with us. I think
I convinced him to stay put until we know more. He
has been so torn! Here's hoping for a good night ahead.
So far, no crying—just sleeping. We will continue to
fight!*

Whatever it takes . . .

Love,

Mom

Unfortunately, even after giving her the big drug and
two doses of her Diazepam (the rescue med we sometimes
used at home to stop a seizure that lasts too long), the
next night, they believed she was having cluster seizures
again, so they gave her four more doses of Diazepam.
After being given this many doses of sedating
medications, Jensyn did not fully wake up for five days.
Five days of me hoping for some interaction. Five days
of waiting and wondering and worrying about my
daughter's brain being mush. Five days until she sort of
came back to us. Including those five days, we were in
the hospital for fourteen days, fighting seizures, a new
movement disorder, and drug withdrawal. We received
the most unsettling news when Dr. Smith came to see
us after the weekend of seizures. He disagreed with what
the weekend team had decided to do, and he said that
these "cluster seizures" that the techs and on-call doctor

said they had seen had not been seizures at all. Nothing makes a mom more nauseated than to hear her daughter was not only being misdiagnosed but had also received big, powerful medications that were being used to treat something she did not have.

Chris returned from Montana while we were still in the hospital. It felt great to have his strength and support after what Jensyn and I had just gone through. We will never fully know what actually happened during this time at the hospital, but we will always wonder. Because when they hooked Jensyn up to oxygen during this stay, they sent her home on oxygen, and even though we hoped she would eventually be strong enough to no longer need it, she was never able to live without it again.

PARTY OF ELEVEN

That summer of 2018 marked a change in Jensyn's health. After the issue with the seizures and being sent home on oxygen, we were beginning to see that we might never get to bring a fully healthy child home from the hospital again, and it was difficult to process that reality. Although the hospital stay in July was rough, August was a special time for our family. Alison, a girl from the first youth group Chris and I helped with, reached out to us. She had become a photographer and offered to do a lifestyle shoot for our family to capture simple moments as we interacted with Jensyn. It was such a generous and thoughtful offer, so we accepted.

A week before the photo shoot was supposed to take place, Max met with Sidney's father to ask for the blessing to marry his daughter. I contacted Alison to see if she would be willing to capture an engagement as part of our lifestyle shoot. Since she had never been asked to photograph an engagement before, she was all in!

While in the Cities for an appointment with Jensyn, I solicited Sidney's help to choose outfits for the family to wear for our photos. I told her I wanted her to find something that matched our aesthetic because we wanted her to be in some pictures with Jensyn, too. She had become such an important part of her life and ours. Since the premise of the photos was to honor our connection with Jensyn, Sidney had no idea we were also setting her up for one of the biggest moments of her life.

The shoot took place late in the afternoon on August 11. Jensyn still needed oxygen most of the time, but we did some of the pictures with her cannula in and some without. When we did the ones without oxygen, we kept a tank nearby and quickly put her back on after the photos were taken. Normally, I have a friend do family pictures each year for our Christmas card, but we had been too scattered to take them in 2016 with the chaos after Jensyn's birth, and in 2017, we resorted to a quick snapshot that had been taken on Jensyn's Dedication Day. This was our first time doing official family photos since becoming a party of ten, and we will always treasure the photos we received.

Each kid got a photo taken individually with Jensyn. She took candids of us interacting as a family and posed shots of us in different groupings. It was this day when

Maci and Sid took the iconic photo we cherish the most. Both girls are holding Jensyn and kissing her cheek. Sheepishly and with an exasperated smirk on her face, Jensyn appears to be merely tolerating their squishing smooches. It captures Jensyn's personality and highlights the great love her sister and soon-to-be sister-in-law had for her. Once we finished all of the family photos, it was time for Max to make his move.

Max asked Alison if she would be willing to take a few pictures of him and Sidney as a couple. She readily agreed to do so. After posing them next to each other and asking them to say "sweet nothings" to each other, she had the two of them do things like share adjectives they would use to describe each other. Then she had Max whisper something in Sidney's ear. She asked them to snuggle in close and take a deep breath simultaneously, recognizing that they were good together. Next, she had them both close their eyes and she told Sidney to put her hand on Max's face and to think about what she most respected about him. Then, she was told to whisper her answer in his ear. Finally, with their eyes still closed, they turned to face each other while holding hands. Max was asked to think about what he most adored about Sidney. When he was ready, he was supposed to give her hands a squeeze and drop to one knee so when she opened her eyes, he would be in position to ask her the ever-important question! None of us had any idea what the two of them were telling each other, but we heard her answer to his question loud and clear. Sidney was a yes to joining our family!

The photos were taken behind our new house and at the park in our neighborhood. We arranged for the proposal to happen at the park so that Sidney's parents could better conceal themselves to witness the moment. After a successful mission, the rest of her family joined us for a spontaneous engagement party. This was a much-needed bright spot in our lives after the hard of the past couple of years. The craziest thing about all of it was that they had their hearts set on a December wedding. It was August. This meant we had four months to pull off something neither family had ever done. Both Sidney and her mother allowed me to take an active role in the planning, for which I was beyond grateful. Organizing brings me joy, and getting to put my passions into planning my firstborn's wedding along with his bride and her mother was more than a joy; it was a gift.

I would love to be able to say that Jensyn rallied and did not require as much attention throughout those four months in the midst of the lists and details of planning a wedding, but sadly, that just was not true. She only spent five days in the hospital in September, but October was more challenging. Jensyn got sick on October 12 and had to stay in the hospital. We figured it was a routine pneumonia—copy and paste, rinse and repeat—and that she would be out within a week. Her seizures amped up a bit, and the doctor wanted to try a new, no-joke, might-make-her-lose-her-vision med. We had exhausted everything else and made the decision that a chance at sight loss (albeit a minor one) was better than no quality of life with her stinking seizures. We agreed to the medicine. She still was not one hundred percent better on the new med, but we all thought it would be fine for her to go home and stay on top of things there.

We went home on a Friday after Jensyn had been in the hospital for a whole week. Our church had given Chris four weeks of sabbatical to rest and refuel for ministry. It was to begin that following Monday. We had planned to go on a cruise during the first week of his sabbatical, another trip I had earned from my sweet side gig. After fewer than twenty-four hours of being at home, we noticed Jensyn was having lots of seizures and was requiring more and more oxygen. We called the epilepsy doctor and were told to take her back immediately. The hospital happened; the cruise did not.

I had never been on a cruise, so I had been really looking forward to that time with Chris. When my kids asked me if I was sad about not getting to go, I told them the truth. It is just a trip, and I would choose any of them over a trip at any time, no matter what. I was not devastated about the trip—I really wasn't. But, I have to admit that some seeds of disbelief were planted in my heart that day: Disbelief that our lives would ever be manageable again. Disbelief that God would ever heal my daughter. Disbelief that God even cared enough to give me the true desires of my heart. This eventually led to a little heart-to-heart between God and me one Sunday morning in early November.

The next time Jensyn was released from the hospital was October 26. Not only did we miss the cruise, but I also missed out on being home with Chris and the kids for the entire first week of his sabbatical. Bitterness was starting to surface, and I struggled to tamp it down. When Chris took the kids to church that following Sunday, I stayed home with Jensyn. At this point, I was pretty closed off to what God wanted in my life because it felt like I had been burned so many times in the past two years. I do not know if I was ever able to fully understand my frustration, but missing the first week of this time with Chris when we were anticipating the BIGGEST moment in our family's lives in December really stung, so I literally and loudly cried out to God.

I told Him that I did not believe He would sustain Jensyn enough to keep her out of the hospital during the rest of Chris's sabbatical so that we could have unfractured time as a family. I declared that I did not believe He would bless our family with Jensyn being healthy for Max's wedding. I cried out that because of Jensyn's previous track record: sixty-one days in the hospital her first year of life and sixty-two days in the hospital so far in her second year of life, I did not believe God would honor my heart's cry to be able to be out of the hospital for the rest of sabbatical and through Max's wedding. I prayed. I cried. I

I NEEDED HIM TO SHOW ME THAT I COULD TRUST HIM AGAIN.

pleaded. I needed Him to show me that I could trust Him again.

At the end of this moment, I wish I could say that He gave me an overwhelming peace—and while it did come, it did not come immediately. In fact, just a week later, Chris and I took Jensyn to see her pulmonologist and were told that she had pneumonia again. Since Chris was not working then, we decided to brave it at home with all of the equipment and meds we had, and we nursed her through this stint together. It seemed she was getting stronger daily, and I was beginning to get some peace. More importantly, my belief that God had heard and listened to my heart's cry for my family was awakening.

We missed that first week of sabbatical, but we were together for the next four weeks including a week of vacation for Thanksgiving! It was such a special time. Even with the chaos of December approaching, my belief was getting stronger. Jensyn was healthy, and my rockstar husband was instrumental in keeping her there. He faithfully spent an hour each morning and night doing her vest treatment, her cough assist, her inhalers, and so much more. I would do her meds and her feeds. Together, we were beginning to discover what it took to stay on top of Jensyn's needs, and I was so very grateful for him.

Jensyn made it through Christmas with not even a sniffle. We needed her to be strong for one more week so she could be at Max's wedding and we could celebrate as a complete family. In my finite mind, I joked with people that I would gladly call the ambulance on December 30 as long as Jensyn was well enough to make it through the wedding on December 29. All weddings are emotional for me, so there were many tears over the weekend, but when I saw Sidney's brother, Owen, pulling Jensyn in her wagon, announcing the bride's coming, my belief in God came full circle. Not only had she remained healthy through the wedding, but she was strong enough that we could take pictures quickly and send her down the aisle without her oxygen. This is a moment in my faith journey I will never forget.

God met me where I was in my unbelief, and He did more than get Jensyn through the wedding. In fact, He kept her out of the hospital until January 25, 2019. God handled my bitterness; He addressed my unbelief. But in His goodness, He did not let my feelings stay there. He restored in me what the previous years had stolen. At my core, I have always believed God can be trusted. Even when put to the test, even when I could not see how He would redeem my anxious, worried, and frenzied soul, He showed up and did what only He could do.

With all we had gone through those first two years, we soon learned that our trust was merely skimming the surface of what we would need going forward. The days were coming when complete confidence in God would be required, days when we would have to make hard decisions, days when we would have to go against what the medical community advised even when the alternative was not the norm. The story God had begun to write was not reading like we had assumed it would, so as a family, we had to edit our responses to adjust for the plot twists that, once again, we could not see coming.

INTUBATED

Jensyn's hospital stint in January was quick—we were only there for two days. Again, seizures were the reason, but it always felt like a small victory when we were discharged quickly. We were hoping for less medical chaos in the coming days, but unfortunately, we found ourselves back in the hospital a month later at the end of February. Just like before, Jensyn got sick quickly. And just when the resident thought it might be okay for us to head home, the rounding doctor, who had been Jensyn's doctor at a previous stay and knew how she rolled, overruled him.

The overnight nurse and I struggled to stay ahead of Jensyn's rising oxygen needs, but at 6:00 a.m., the nurse called the doctor, and the doctor called Rapid Response. Rapid Response is a team that comes quickly from the ICU when summoned, and within no time at all, Jensyn was transferred to the PICU. Just a few hours later, Jensyn had her first blood transfusion, and a breathing tube was put in. Chris and I did not have time to question things or make a decision. Jensyn decided for us.

We had seen Jensyn struggle when she was sick in the past, but seeing the drastic measures needed for her to fight for her life and the subsequent comatose state it put her in was more than we could comprehend. Everything happened so fast. And then time stood still.

February 22, 2019

Well, you fought hard, but your sweet body was exhausted. Yesterday, after we heard you had a fairly uneventful night, we were hopeful you had turned a corner. But you were struggling again just minutes after we got to your room. Your blood gasses are too high, and your pH is not in a safe range. They told us you had to have a breathing tube. There was no other choice. Dad and I had to leave the room while they sedated you and put in the tube. They also had to put a central line in your neck. It was so hard to see your air hunger this morning as you were trying to breathe, but it is equally hard to see you just lying there with a machine breathing for you. We are hopeful this will make all the difference and that you will rebound from this quickly. It will take a few days for your body to settle in and fight the infection in your lungs. We will

*be with you through it all and will do whatever we
need to do.*

Whatever it takes . . .
Love,
Mom

Even though Jensyn had been in the ICU at birth
and one time later in Minneapolis, we did not know what
being on a breathing tube entailed. During this stay, we
learned that the patient had to be kept in a sedated state
so that they would not fight the tube. This is where the
term "medically induced coma" comes in. Perhaps they
should have just given her a bunch of seizure meds—those
knocked her out for days! All joking aside, the lethargy and
listlessness were hard to see, but even more difficult was
witnessing what happened when the sedation meds wore
off a bit. She would hold her breath, causing her oxygen
to dip into the 30s and 40s. Nurses would have to use an
Ambu bag (a bag attached to a mask that delivers positive
pressure ventilation to someone who is struggling to
breathe) to help get her lungs to recruit necessary air.
They would then give her a bump of the sedation meds,
and she would return to the Land of the Loopy. She was
on the ventilator for fourteen days and in the hospital
for nine more days until we took Jensyn home on March
16, just one day shy of a complete month. Obviously, she

shattered her previous stay record, which was the most difficult stay to date, but we had hope that she would fully recover at home.

This record stay was at St. Paul Children's, so we had our first experience in their PICU. It is a smaller hospital, with only twelve rooms on the ICU floor. There is a Ronald McDonald area at this hospital as well, but it is not as big and exists primarily for meals, laundry, and a lounge to relax in. Instead of having overnight rooms like the Minneapolis Ronald has, St. Paul is set up differently. When a child is on the critical care floor, there are "sleep rooms" available for the families. They are not part of the Ronald McDonald area. Instead, they are down the hall and just outside the intensive care unit. Each room has two beds and either an attached bathroom or a bathroom that is shared between two rooms. They are less luxurious than the rooms in Minneapolis, but they became a true blessing for us during our extended stays at St. Paul Children's. I would spend my days bedside with Jensyn, but at the end of the day, it was a blessing to head to a quiet room—no beeps or alarms or machines—to recharge and regroup for the next day.

As with most stays, I would go home for a night here or there, but for the most part, I would remain at the hospital with Jensyn for the duration. Chris would come whenever he could, and our parents would switch off staying with the other kids. Obviously, our older kids could have managed things at home, but we believed that was too much pressure to put on them with how frequent these stays were.

Throughout it all, I continued to homeschool the kids. Chris would bring my lesson planning notebooks to the hospital on the weekend and then take them home so the kids would know what to complete for their weekly assignments. Often, a nurse or doctor would come in during a Facetime lesson I would be having with one or two of the kids. For sure, we did not get to do all of the things I had planned for their school days, but they did their math, their language arts, and whatever they needed to do for their co-op classes. They were undoubtedly learning life skills as more was expected of each of them around the house and as they cared for each other.

Leaving Jensyn alone while she was inpatient was never an option we entertained. Both Chris and I believed someone needed to be with her at all times. It was not because we did not trust the people attending to her care; she had the best of the best. It was also not because Jensyn demanded that we stay, even though we absolutely believed she knew if we were there. It was important to us because Jensyn could not speak for herself, and nobody knew her better than we did. Even when Chris's grandpa passed away, my mom stayed at the hospital with

Jensyn so that I could attend the funeral with my family. Although I would sometimes sleep in a different room, I was always in the building. Jensyn was never alone; the entire family agreed this was how it should be.

Spending so much time in the hospital with Jensyn wore on me, but it also allowed me to form unique connections with the doctors and nurses. When I say they were the best of the best, I am not kidding. Not only did I enjoy these new relationships but Jensyn had become someone special to them. There was just something about her. She never said a word, but the nurses came to know our girl over the years. Since we were such "frequent fliers," we often had the same nurses, we got to know many of the doctors and intensivists, and there were even a few nursing assistants who would brighten our days when they popped in to check on Jensyn or say hello to me. Since they all worked so closely together, they were like family, and we were lucky enough to be welcomed into that family. It felt like they were just as invested as we were in helping Jensyn get and stay well.

Unfortunately, just a month after being home from the twenty-nine-day stay, Jensyn returned to the PICU. This time, she most likely had contracted a new virus that stirred up the bacteria still in her lungs from the previous month, and this bacteria was ready to party again! Rarely was she ever on a regular floor again, and every time after this visit, our goal was to avoid the breathing tube. We managed to dodge it this time, even though we were in the hospital for another fifteen days.

Apparently, once a complex child like Jensyn has been on a breathing tube, the red flags go off in the palliative care world. Earlier in her journey, we had met with a palliative care doctor and his team. Before meeting with them, I had to look up the meaning of "palliative" just to educate myself. What I discovered, I did not like. When Jensyn's pulmonologist suggested that she connect us with them, I remember thinking we would do whatever it took to help Jensyn, yet when I realized what they were about, it was another time in this journey where I could not reconcile their truth with my reality.

Palliative care focuses on maintaining a patient's quality of life while managing treatment and other needs. That sounds like a good thing, right? But as I looked into it, I realized that a healthy person does not need a palliative care team. They see terminal, critical patients. Often, it has been defined to me as one step below hospice, and I understand the role hospice plays.

When Chris and I took Jensyn to our first appointment with palliative care, it was unsettling in so many ways. At this point, we had accepted that Jensyn would not live a full and healthy life, but this team of medical professionals seemed to want us to put a timeline on what we would be willing to endure. They wanted to know when we would be okay with making the ever-difficult decision that it was time to let Jensyn go. Huh? I thought we would be meeting about how they could help us maintain a good quality of life for Jensyn—being proactive, setting goals, and figuring out next steps for her to be comfortable. Instead, they wanted to know if we believed Jensyn was suffering and if we had ever heard of a POLST (Provider Orders for Life-Sustaining Treatment), an advanced care plan that identifies our end-of-life medical treatment wishes. Ultimately, their advice was to make plans ahead so that we would not have to decide whether or not to let her go in the middle of a crisis.

Oh, how we hated this appointment. Of course, talking about our daughter not living forever is hard enough, but that was not the part that bothered us. It was that other people questioned Jensyn's quality of life and the value she added to our family. Jensyn was not a decision that had to be made. She suffered when she was sick, but so do I. When she was well, she added joy to our family like no other child or sibling had.

Our eyes were suddenly wide open to a world where life was not always valued, where someone could just be "let go" because they were sick or had become a burden on the family. I had never believed this type of "health" care existed, but now I know it does. And I could not handle it. We told that counselor that God would make it abundantly clear to us when Jensyn was ready to go home, and we never wavered from that belief.

After her palliative doctor visited us in the hospital during this stay, I wrote this on Jensyn's CaringBridge site:

April 16, 2019

Yesterday, we had a visit from Jensyn's palliative care doctor. He asked if we had thought any more about what we would do if Jensyn had another long hospital stay or if she ever needed to be intubated again. He asked around the edges, but he was really saying that it would be okay for us to let our daughter go if that were to happen again. It is terrifying to think this would ever be a decision someone would have to make. I know he was just doing his job, but I am not sure this is a doctor we need for our team. Chris and I have no intentions of ever not fighting for our daughter. It is our prayer that God will intervene when and if this becomes an issue. These are hard situations, but we know that we can trust God through it all.

We severed ties with this particular doctor after our hospital stay. Looking back, we were not ready for the services of this team, just like we would never be ready to do what they suggested we do. Later in our journey, we were open to the comfort measures that palliative care can provide, and at that time, we resumed our connection with them. Jensyn got a new doctor, and even

CHANGE WAS
BECOMING TOO
MUCH FOR ME.

though we did not always agree with the advice this doctor gave, she understood how we viewed our daughter and was willing to support us in that.

At the end of her fifteen days, Jensyn was sent home with her very own BiPAP machine. This machine helped push air into her lungs—positive pressure ventilation—and the hope was that if she used it at night and when she was starting to get sick, it would strengthen her weak lungs. Another machine! Although it was useful and became an essential part of Jensyn's routine, the fact that it needed to be used daily was just another indication of her declining health.

We celebrated Maci's high school graduation three weeks after Jensyn left the hospital. As always, our goal was for Jensyn to be healthy enough for these big family events, so we were thrilled she could party with us. Just a week later, Maci moved to Ensenada, Mexico, to do a Discipleship Training School with Youth With A Mission (YWAM). Her long-term plan was to live there as a missionary. My mama's heart was proud and so excited for her, but again, I felt loss by letting my oldest girl move so far away. With each child who left, the family dynamic changed. Change was becoming too much for me.

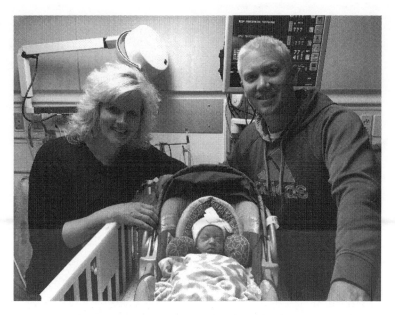

Breaking out of our first NICU stay.

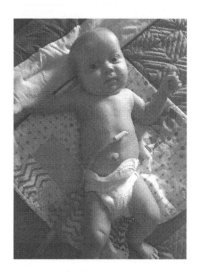

Jensyn's first
button contraption.

Jensyn loved
her NICU family.

Jensyn's unique mode of emergency transport.

Nothing better
than a Jensyn grin.

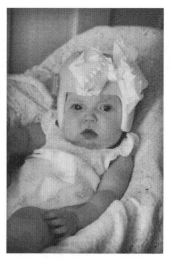

Rocking her
sassy pink helmet.

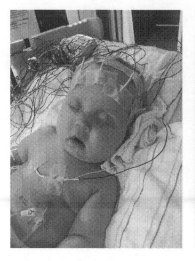

One of many EEGs
and her rainbow extensions.

Chris's signature cuddle
with his girl.

Iconic photo from our lifestyle shoot.

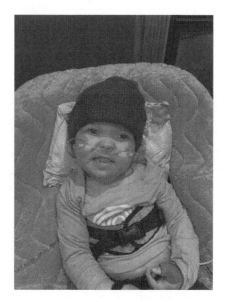

Family Fave Photo—best personality.

The three of us.

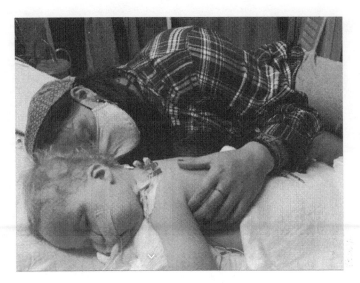

Maci made it in time from Mexico in 2020.

When Jensyn fought death the first time in 2020.

Maci and Chase's Wedding.

The bride with her flowergirl.

Britlyn loves her Jensyn.

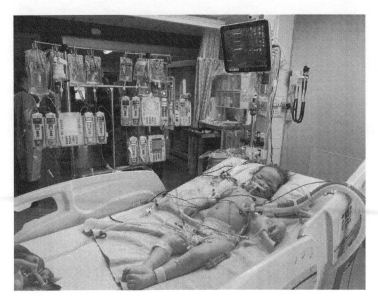

When Jensyn fought death for the second time in 2022.

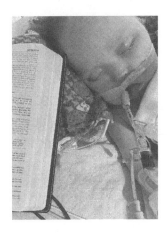

Even while intubated, the Gospel affected Jensyn.

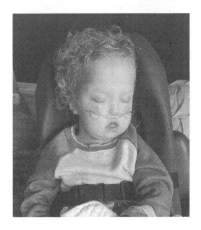

Our sleepy sloth did life with her eyes closed.

Jensyn starts Kindergarten.

One last photo together before we ushered Jensyn
into the arms of Jesus.

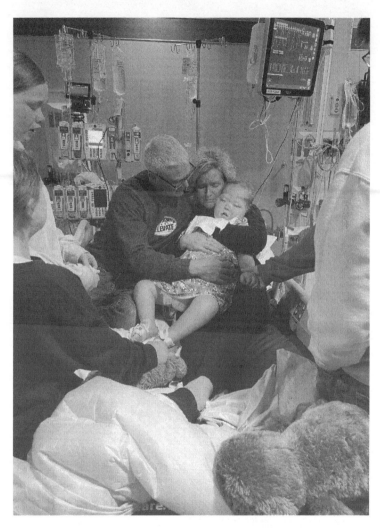

Untethered—The last time Chris and I held Jensyn
on this side of heaven.

Our first family photo without Jensyn—Haven, Sidney, Crosby, Max, Sadie, Tygen, Chase, Judah, Maci. Brinkley, Kristin, Chris, Tate. Britlyn, Latte, Jakely.

A family who grieves together, tattoos together.

A FAMILY OF NURSES

The unspoken truth within our family is that even though Jensyn needed lots of interventions and medical attention, we all believed she would, at some point, get healthier and stronger. As time passed, Jensyn was still in and out of the hospital on a consistent basis. We did what we could at home to keep her away from germs and viruses, and in a way, we continued to watch her slowly lose more and more of herself. Yet, we never questioned her worth or her place in our family. Jensyn just required more, and it was a privilege to care for her and meet her needs. Sometimes, it felt like we were just keeping her alive, but providing for her and serving her created a bond in our family that was unbreakable and absolutely beautiful.

When Jensyn's waiver was renewed in January 2019, we learned that Jensyn was fragile enough to qualify for a full-time nurse. I was not sure how to feel about that.

It would be nice to have the extra help, but I could not imagine having another stranger in our home, let alone one who would be there for twelve hours a day. We were told we could choose to have the nurse come during the day or overnight, whichever would help us most. Overnight? While we were sleeping? An invited stranger in our home? Um, no. We were not ready for that. But we agreed to try having a nurse during the day.

Even though Sidney was still working with Jensyn, it was appealing to know that someone else could help with her treatments and other needs. We decided to bring on a nurse, who the county found for us. Our first nurse was Florence, and she was a wonderful woman with a loving and caring demeanor. Her Liberian accent was strong, so communication was difficult at times, but she took such great care of Jensyn and was so kind to the rest of the kids as well. We were thrilled with our first experience of having a nurse in the home. Unfortunately, after having her for about a month, our insurance company informed us she was out of network. This meant we had to look for someone else, which we were sad about because we really enjoyed Florence.

With the shortage of nurses, we did not find another one until November 2019, when Shanna came to work for us. Shanna had just graduated from nursing school and was looking for a job. Even though she was young and fresh out of college, she jumped right in and took great care of Jensyn. The family grew to love having her in the home, and we were sad when she left us in March 2020 for a job in Rochester, but we understood it was a smart career move for her.

Fortunately, a new nurse was ready to take over when Shanna left. Chris already knew Denice from ministry work he had done with her in the past, so when she offered to help us care for Jensyn, she was not a total stranger to our family. Denice had been a nurse for many years and had experience with kids and adults. Even while working with Jensyn, she was also serving hospice patients. Compassion, empathy, and love run deep with Denice, so we knew we had found a perfect fit for our daughter. We even felt comfortable having Denice in the house overnight when we needed her, so that was a win. It was also a bonus that she was planning to stay with us for the long haul, and we would find in time that she would become more than a nurse to us for the rest of Jensyn's days—she became part of our family.

Even with the outside help our family received to care for Jensyn, most of her care remained a family affair. In fact, Sidney was so invested in serving Jensyn that she drove from St. Paul, where she and Max were living on campus in married housing. She worked three days a week for eight hours a day and would help on the weekends as needed. Tygen took over Maci's hours when she moved to Mexico. He would cover for me if I had errands to run or appointments and could not be home in time to give Jensyn her meds or do her treatments. He also learned how to mix the formula of her keto ratio, and he took over that daily task. Max often could not physically be with us to help with his sister because of school or work, but I cannot recall a time when I was at the hospital that he did not reach out via text or phone call. He always checked in to see how Jensyn was, but often he was more concerned with how I was doing. It was such a sweet touch of love when his text read: "How are YOU doing, Mom?" This was a tangible way he made sure that we stayed connected through it all, and it meant so much to me.

The other kids also found ways that they could show care for Jensyn. Each of them knew how her machines worked, and they mostly knew what to do if something was alarming or if she was fussing. Tate and Brinkley loved to help us bathe Jensyn. It took at least two people to get her ready to take a bath, which was one of her favorite things to do. Either Chris or I would carry Jensyn upstairs to the master bathroom while someone else carried up her oxygen tank. The kids would rotate, being able to don a swimsuit to get in the jacuzzi tub to hold Jensyn during her bath. This was cherished time with their sister because we often would get the best responses from her while she was in the water. Jakely loved to get Jensyn dressed whenever she could, and reading to her or watching cartoons with her were highlights of special time spent together.

Another area where Jensyn's waiver changed was the addition of a housekeeper. Amy, a friend from church, and her daughter, Natalie, cleaned for us for the first year, but during the COVID-19 pandemic, she could not continue. The next year, we asked Chris's mom if she would like the job, and she agreed to come every other week for us. It was such a help to know that our home was being cleaned regularly. This helped eliminate germs and junk for Jensyn, and it freed Chris and me up to be able to better meet the other needs Jensyn had. It was such a blessing to have this help.

As wonderful as it was to have these types of support, Chris and I did our best to divvy up the needs and cares of Jensyn, Britlyn, and the rest of the kids at home. Our days were like a dance, choreographed to a specific routine. Chris would get up early to get Britlyn off to school while I would get ready for the day. He faithfully did Jensyn's morning treatments and got her food pumping. I would crush and administer her meds. He went to work while I homeschooled the kids. After school, we would manage whatever might be going on with sports, activities, meetings, and outings. One of us would cuddle Britlyn at bedtime, and the other would do Jensyn's nighttime meds and treatments. As Jensyn got older, her needs grew, and her health became more demanding. Yet, there was never a time when any of us believed she was a burden. Serving her was always a privilege—even when the demands of caring for her were about to be tested beyond what we could ever imagine.

THE HARDEST AND BEST

2020. The year the entire world went crazy. The time when nobody knew how life was supposed to work. The days that lasted forever and the moments that became weird, unexpected memories. That time when all of my kids, even my adult children, lived under one roof again and when our family learned what it meant to cherish each second, to fight for each breath. The months where we experienced the scare of loss—not once, but twice. It was a year we will never forget.

Social distancing. Perhaps it was actually defined in March 2020 when the world was put on hold because of the coronavirus, but our family had been social distancing long before then. Since the day when Jensyn's pulmonologist told us to keep her away from groups of people, we social distanced. So, while others learned how to navigate this new concept of steering clear of each

WE RAMPED UP OUR COVERAGE AND KEPT AS MUCH DISTANCE FROM KNOWN DANGER AS POSSIBLE.

other to avoid a virus, our family had already mastered it. Yet, it still felt weird.

Since one of Jensyn's biggest struggles was respiratory issues, a bug like the coronavirus was beyond scary. Although medical professionals said it affected the elderly more often than children, it was scary to imagine what could happen if Jensyn got it. We ramped up our coverage and kept as much distance from known danger as possible. Denice continued to work with Jensyn during this uncertain time, and because schools were sending kids home and colleges were shutting down, Max decided to move home, bringing his new wife with him. Not only did this work great for Sidney as she continued working with Jensyn but it was safer for her because she was newly pregnant with our first grandbaby. Grateful for our bigger home for such a time as this, we were thrilled they could move in with us.

In February, after several weeks at home, Maci returned to Mexico to continue her missionary work. This time, she was fulfilling her requirements to become part of the staff at the YWAM base. Unfortunately, in March, the base decided it was the safest decision to send all their students and staff home until a more settled time. Maci was crushed. There was no indication of when she would get to return to Mexico, and she loved it there so much. Coming home felt defeating to her, but she knew she needed to get home before they shut down the border.

Because of the unknown severity of this virus and since she was coming from outside the country, health officials suggested that anyone in this situation should be quarantined for two weeks. We did not know how to handle Maci's return. We believed that the risk to Jensyn and even to Sidney's unborn baby was too great. Since Max still rented his campus apartment in Roseville, Minnesota, he arranged for Maci and her best friend, Abby (who was also returning from Mexico with her), to stay there. It did not take long for them to get bored and homesick. They did not want to be back in Minnesota in the first place, but being displaced from their homes added a level to their frustration. We also did not like having Maci so far away and worried about her getting sick as well. All that was happening was getting ridiculous. We wanted her with us. After a week, we decided that she had spent enough time in quarantine, so she moved home. Eleven people under one roof might feel overwhelming and chaotic to most, but to me it felt like a gift. We did what we could to pass the time—good food, a tournament of board games, and lots of movies and reality television. We only left the house if we really needed to. The rest of the time, we were together.

Obviously, continuing to homeschool was easy. When the public schools shut down and sent everyone home, Britlyn was also home with us every day. Distance learning became a thing, and while many claimed that distance learning was basically homeschooling, I disagreed. Nope! Nothing like it at all. There are no time parameters with homeschooling, no hoops to jump through. With distance learning, Britlyn had to be on her iPad at certain times throughout the day and was required to complete different tasks and assignments. Because learning is a challenge for her on a normal day, she needed someone else to be with her when she was "doing school" at home, which added stress to our days. I do not think she learned much, academically speaking, the rest of that year, but since we were all in survival mode, it did not matter much.

I wish I could say that Jensyn remained healthy throughout this threatening time, but she did get sick even with our best efforts to keep her healthy. We were hearing stories of loved ones not being able to be at the hospital with their sick family members, which was too scary to even imagine. During this time, we had our first exposure to telemedicine appointments where we could "visit" our doctors online. Clinics were closed, and hospitals were not taking patients for non-essential reasons, so this became our next best option. When Jensyn first got sick, we connected with her pulmonologist, who prescribed a steroid burst and around-the-clock treatments. It was a blessing to have Sidney and Maci living with us because they often took shifts so that Chris and I would not have to do it all alone. Denice would come during the day to give us a break as well. It truly was a team effort. We enacted Operation Keep Jensyn Home, and everyone did their part to fulfill that mission.

These were strange and unsettling days. The one constant thing we had was each other. Chris and I tried to make the days meaningful and somewhat fun. Each day during lunch, Chris asked the kids a question to spark some meaningful discussion. One day, he inquired, "What is the hardest thing our family has ever gone through?" The answer was quick and certain: "Jensyn." We hated that Jensyn struggled and never seemed to get a break from feeling lousy. Each of us wanted her to have an easier life, one that was not consumed with hospitals and sickness and weakness and uncertainty. As the discussion continued, the consensus was not that life *with* Jensyn was hard. Rather, life *for* Jensyn was hard, and because of our great love for her, we *felt* that hard.

The next day at lunch, Chris posed another question: "What is the best thing that has ever happened to our family?" Again, the answer was resolute and resolved:

"Jensyn." No doubt, no discussion. This was not the answer we expected, but what we had known since she was born was being solidified in our hearts and before our eyes—there was something special about this girl. The hardest and the best. A gift only God can define. Being likeminded in our love for Jensyn created a solid foundation, which was good because it would soon be rattled.

NAVIGATING PANDEMIC PANDEMONIUM

Even with increased care and all-in efforts, Jensyn did earn a trip to the hospital at the end of April 2020. It was a short stay and had more to do with seizures and the fact that we had used her rescue medication at home. We knew the valium in this medication was super sedating to her, but we had no choice. We had to stop the seizures. In return, it caused her to be super sleepy, and as a result, her oxygen needs increased. After meeting virtually with her pediatrician and epilepsy doctor, they suggested we take her to the emergency room for a consultation.

In a way, we were curious about what would happen at the hospital during the pandemic. We were the only people in the waiting room (that had never happened) and were taken back to a room quickly. When they took Jensyn off our home oxygen to put her on hospital oxygen, she tanked so quickly that they immediately moved us to a room in a new respiratory wing of the ED. This room was isolated and equipped for contagion. Jensyn was always a hard stick for an IV, so it took them a while to find a vein (six attempts). During all this, they quickly gave her a COVID-19 test and had it couriered over to Minneapolis for results. Apparently, even though we were not concerned about her having the virus, it was now standard procedure for kids like her to be tested immediately. After we learned the test was negative, we were allowed to go to a room on a regular floor. This did not decrease the need for all medical staff to wear full garb, along with a face mask and a helmet with a shield. The atmosphere felt so weird compared to our previous hospital experiences. Luckily, Chris and I were allowed to stay with her, and nobody asked us to wear a mask. Oh, the inconsistencies!

Fortunately, we were only inpatient for seven days; unfortunately, the Jensyn we took home was not entirely well. Something I wrote in her journal entry on the last day of this stay was beginning to be true for us on every discharge day.

April 27, 2020

We are busting out of here today! Dad is on his way to get us. I do not believe we are taking home a super healthy girl, but what they are doing here, we can continue at home. So, we are going to go for it. Between Sid, Maci, Denice, Dad, and me, we should be able to help you regain some strength and lung function. For now, it is a waiting game. I am glad we get to do it at home so that we can be with the others. It is where we belong.

Whatever it takes . . .
Love you, sweet girl,
Mom

Each time we left the hospital, it seemed there was more healing for Jensyn to do. In previous stays, the doctors began to ask me if *I* was ready to take Jensyn home, if *I* believed I could take over what they were doing. If so, they were willing to discharge us. Sometimes, I was not confident in our collaborative ability to maintain her cares; other times, I knew we could. This was one of those times when I believed that home was better for her than the hospital, so they set us free.

Strange things continued to happen around our world and even more in our state. The end of May was tumultuous in Minnesota after the death of George Floyd and the subsequent violence that ensued. Nothing felt normal, but life continued to move forward. In June, shortly after the riots in Minneapolis, Jensyn gave us our first real emergent scare. She had been developing a cold for a few days, but we believed we could stay ahead of her needs. It was the weekend, and Sid and I had done what we could to keep her comfortable on Friday and Saturday. Saturday night, Jensyn was getting gunkier and needed more oxygen. She also required more suctioning to keep her airways clear. Chris was supposed to preach that next morning, so I agreed to bunk in with Jensyn to better observe her needs. It was a good thing I was with her because she continued to struggle, and I spent the entire night chasing her secretions and switching out her oxygen tanks. We had an oxygen concentrator that delivered nonstop oxygen, but it topped out at five liters. That night, Jensyn required eight liters. This meant I had to use oxygen tanks, which would only last about an hour before I would have to get a new one.

We made it through the night, and Denice took over in the morning so I could go to church to hear Chris preach. Denice felt confident Jensyn would be okay while I was at church; however, when I got home, it was apparent that her needs were more significant than we could manage. We called 911 for transport, and Denice felt Jensyn was critical enough that she should accompany us on the trip. She rode in the back with the medic, and I rode shotgun with the other EMT. They had Jensyn stabilized, so I enjoyed chatting with the gal who was driving. She told me about her previous days when she and the other EMTs were on the scene in downtown Minneapolis during the riots. She pointed out the many buildings that had burned down, some of which we could see as we drove by. Everything felt so weird.

When we were about thirty minutes from the hospital, we heard Jensyn coughing and gagging while Denice and the medic suctioned her. The EMT yelled to the front, "We're struggling back here. Let's light it up!" Once the sirens were on, I began to worry. Had we waited too long? Was she going to be okay? I texted Chris to tell him to start driving and to meet us at the hospital. When we got to the ED, a dozen people met us at the door and quickly began working on Jensyn. They got the IV in with one poke, which never happened, and they began to run all the tests. There was such a flurry of activity I could not even be in the room with her. Then, Denice told me her oxygen had gotten as low as 60 at one point. We were hardly in the ED before they moved us to the PICU. At this point, Jensyn was on ten liters of oxygen and full BiPap. The ICU doctor said an intubation was not out of the question. Jensyn was suddenly very sick.

Ironically, this was another seven-day stay, and even more bizarre is that when we took Jensyn home this time, she was healthier and seemed to have gotten back some of her chatter and strength.

June 22, 2020

We get to go home today! A week's stay is not very long for you. So grateful things went the way they did instead of you needing more intervention. The nurses who had you last Monday marvel at how well you are doing now. They were all afraid that you would be sicker than you were. Of course, we know there is an insane number of people praying for you. There is no doubt that prayer plays a huge role in your recovery.

Whatever it takes . . .
Let's go home and stay home!
Love,
Mom

Jensyn's team of prayer warriors was enormous. People we had not spoken to in years followed our story. New friends rallied with encouragement and support. Our church family continually stormed the gates of heaven on our family's behalf. We felt it. We never doubted it. And we shared it with the doctors and nurses whenever we could. They knew Jensyn was prayed for and that God was doing something special in her life and through her story. I think this is why I was always baffled when someone questioned the choices we were making.

At one point during the summer of 2020, Jensyn was struggling again and needed more oxygen. Denice mentioned that getting an oxygen concentrator that could do more than five liters was possible. When I called Pediatric Home Services (our medical supply company), they said I would need a doctor's order to be able to get one. I used the portal to message Jensyn's pulmonologist to inquire about this possibility. Within minutes, my phone rang. Expecting it to be a nurse,

"HOW MUCH LONGER ARE YOU GOING TO SUFFER?"

I was surprised that it was actually her pulmonologist calling instead. She asked what caused me to inquire about a stronger machine. I said that I wanted more options, that often Jensyn needed just a little bit more than the five liters, and that it is not feasible to rely on oxygen tanks when she needs more. There was a pause, and then she asked, "How much longer are you planning to do this, Kristin?"

I was confused. "How much longer am I planning to do what?" I asked.

"How much longer are you going to suffer? How much longer is your family going to suffer? And Jensyn? How much more do you think she can take?"

I was shocked. What did she mean? She explained that she could continue giving us more machines and tools, but at what cost? Again, she asked, "How much longer are you going to keep this going?"

Now, I was mad and could hardly articulate my thoughts in full sentences. "We are not suffering. Jensyn is not suffering. Losing Jensyn would cause my kids to suffer. Jensyn is the best thing that ever happened to us, and we will *keep this going* as long as we need to."

At this point, I was crying and obviously upset. I do not think the pulmonologist knew how to handle my response, and I cannot remember much from the rest of the call. Ultimately, she decided that if Jensyn needed more than the five liters, we should continue doing what we had been doing and take her to the hospital. She did not agree to give us the new machine, and I could not wait to get off the phone. Chris came home to a distraught wife.

This marked another time in our journey when someone did not see the same value in Jensyn as we did. This is the same specialist who connected us with palliative. In hindsight, I realize she was often more concerned with how Chris and I were doing than with Jensyn. At first, I believed that to be nurturing and kind. But I was beginning to see who she really was, and with her, my guard was up.

EXPLODED

I t was the fall of 2020. We had made it through the summer, and a new school year was beginning. Maci had returned to Mexico in late June, and Max and Sidney moved into their new apartment just fifteen minutes away. Sidney's commute to work with Jensyn was much more doable than her hour-long trip from the Twin Cities. Things felt like they were returning to normal— well, except that public school was unpredictable. Since distance learning had been a train wreck for Britlyn and because there was no guarantee that school would remain in-person for the entire year, we decided to bring Britlyn home to join our homeschool. It was another time of transition for our family, but we were hopeful things were about to level out.

But then came August 30. We had just taken back-to-school photos of the kids, and I was preparing to go to a friend's house for supper. I remember my phone ringing, and I knew it was Maci calling, but I did not get to it in time to take her call. The next thing I remember was Chris coming downstairs to find me, and I could hear a very panicked Maci on the phone. She was ballistic! She could hardly speak complete sentences and was trying to articulate what had happened through tears and absolute hysteria.

"My apartment blew up! It's on fire! There was a gas leak. Ashley was napping in my room! I got her out. I lost everything! Ashley is burned bad! I don't know if she will be okay," Maci yelled. "Mom! It was so scary!"

"Are you okay?" we asked.

"I think so," she said. "I cut my foot, but I did not get burned. But, Ashley! It is not good, Mom! She was right where the fire was and she got so burned and she did not wake up when I called her. I knew I had to get to her and I had to pry open the wall and I got her, but I am so scared for her."

Obviously, we were so grateful that Maci was okay enough to call us, but it was challenging to be so far away. How could we support our daughter after such a massive scare when we were not able to be with her? The details were scattered and sketchy, and these unknowns left us in our own state of shock and confusion.

As the story unfolded over the next few days, we learned that Maci and her roommate had recently moved to a new apartment just a few blocks from the YWAM base in Ensenada. Her roommate had found this new apartment while Maci was doing staff training in Tijuana. It was less expensive and closer to the base, and because the law required a native landowner to co-sign a lease, Maci's roommate took care of the details. By the time Maci returned from Tijuana, she had lived in the new apartment for only three days before the explosion. It happened on a Sunday afternoon. Maci's friend, Ashley, was visiting for the day. The night before, Ashley had been out late at a wedding, so she had asked Maci if she could take a quick nap in her room. Maci and two other friends were hanging out in the living room area, just outside the room where Ashley was napping.

Throughout the afternoon, the smell of gas became quite strong. Earlier that day, someone had come to hook up their washer and dryer, which was located in the back of their apartment, adjacent to Maci's bedroom. Since the guy had been there that morning, the girls believed the smell was so strong because things had just been hooked up. They were only in the apartment for an hour and a half when the explosion happened. The two girls with Maci ran out the front door, and once Maci got her bearings, she remembered that Ashley was napping in her room.

The explosion had moved the bed in front of the bedroom door, so Maci had to pry open part of the wall to get to her friend. Ashley was badly burned—over forty-nine percent of her body—but Maci was able to get her out to the street, where she met another friend who drove her to the hospital. After the fire department arrived, the girls could see the extent of their reality. Since the explosion happened at the back of the building and Maci's room was next to the laundry area, she lost everything she owned.

Chris and I realized we could have received a very different phone call that day. Not only was our daughter alive, but she was not at all burned or even badly injured—the only physical issue was the glass in her foot from a shattered window. Emotionally, however, she was a mess.

A few days after the explosion, we learned about the legal ramifications of this situation. Apparently, since the renter is responsible for finding the person to hook up any appliances, it becomes the renter's responsibility to pay for any issues. This meant that Maci, her roommate, and the landowner who co-signed were responsible for the losses and damages to the building and for Ashley's medical care. Not wanting Maci to navigate all this alone, Chris and I decided to fly to Ensenada to be with our girl. A simple decision turned out to be another test of our trust.

Before leaving, we had a handful of people text or call us, questioning what we were doing. They said things like, "It sounds like a bad movie," and "You owe a lot of money—what if they detain you?" or "If it were my

daughter, I would just go get her and get her out of there."
"Is it wise for both of you to go?" Aside from the many
concerns for our safety, the biggest obstacle was flying
during the pandemic. Because of the virus, Chris had not
been able to renew his driver's license or passport, and we
planned to cross the border and leave our country. What
if they would not let him back in? As we prepared to go,
obstacles continued to stack against us, but we knew we
had to get there for Maci. Leaving Jensyn offered its own
set of issues and concerns, but we could always count on
Sidney to care for her around the clock when we needed
her to do so. When we reached the border, they stopped
the car in front of us. Afraid of what this might mean for
us, we saw God at work when they waved our vehicle
through the border without stopping us.

We stayed in Ensenada with Maci for a little over
a week. During that time, we continued to see God do
things only He can do. The landowner and his wife were
so gracious and forgiving about everything. We were
with Maci when she went back to see the wreckage for
the first time—a total loss—yet even in the midst of the
destruction, Maci found her Bible. It was wet, and the
edges were singed, but we could still read the words. What
a treasure to see that God's Word was preserved even in
this. We also were able to help Maci shop for some basic
things she needed. Over and over, we saw other people
reaching out to Maci and blessing her with clothing

and money, replacing her laptop and guitar. Many cared for Maci and helped her navigate life in response to all she had gone through. Of course, we offered for her to come home with us, but she always felt closest to Jesus in Mexico, so we trusted God and let her stay.

Maci's main concern continued to be Ashley. The majority of Ashley's burns were on her arms, hands, legs, and feet, with her arms and hands being the worst. When she was first burned, doctors had no idea if she would ever regain full use of her hands or how bad the scarring would be. Fortunately, the COVID-19 restrictions in Mexico were not as severe as in the United States. One of Ashley's parents (who lived in Queretaro, Mexico) was able to be with her at all times, and often Maci and other friends were permitted to visit her as well.

While we were in Mexico, several people shared how brave Maci was to carry Ashley out of the building. When I asked Maci about this, she said, "Well, it was more of a dragging, Mom, but I had to get her out of there." I like to think that I would have been strong enough to get my friend out of a burning building, but I cannot say for sure what I would have done in a situation like that. It still amazes me that God gave Maci the strength to pry open the wall (I saw the evidence) and also protected both girls in the process.

When it was time to come home, Chris's expired passport and driver's license were not an issue. Again, through all this, we saw that God can be trusted. I was so glad we were nearing the end of 2020 because it sure had been a doozy. It could not possibly get worse, could it?

EXCEEDING EXPECTATIONS

A t this point, nothing in life felt easy. There was a constant feeling of "what's next?" like we were living with a sense of dread. It is hard to explain how it hovered, but it hovered nonetheless. Tygen's sixteenth birthday was approaching, and I had arranged with some of his friends to attempt a surprise party. The plan was to have all his friends come to our house after church on Wednesday night. Once youth group was over, Tygen would come home to a party he did not know about! I love stuff like this and could not wait to bless our boy.

The day before the planned party was pretty typical. Jensyn was getting a cold, but Sidney and I watched her closely. Chris came home while I was making supper and went to Jensyn's room to check on her. He yelled for me to come see Jensyn because he thought she was struggling. I had just been in there a half an hour before, had been checking on her throughout the day, and had not been concerned. However, when I saw her this time, she was obviously not doing as well as I had thought. She was super spitty and lethargic. We knew we needed to call 911. She had been sort of sick in the morning and throughout the day, but now she was really struggling. It came on so fast!

As the EMTs were preparing to get Jensyn on the stretcher and I was rushing around to pack all my things, Tygen came home from football practice. Teary, I told him how sorry I was to be taking her in when his big birthday was the next day. In typical Tygen fashion, he told me not to worry about it and hugged me. I said goodbye to the rest of the crew and hustled outside. This time, when I got in the ambulance, the EMT called a Code 3—we were lights and sirens before we even left our cul-de-sac! I always hated it when they did this because it concerned the kids so much.

When we got to the hospital, a team was waiting for us at the door, ready to do whatever was needed. Unfortunately, Jensyn had gotten worse in transit, so within minutes, they intubated her. Of course, I was shocked. Earlier in the day, she was just developing a cold; it never crossed my mind that we could reach this extreme so quickly. Even though Jensyn had been intubated before, it was still scary. We soon found ourselves in Room 2 of the PICU and had zero idea how long we would be there.

Of course, Tygen's birthday was the next day. I contacted the girls who were helping me with his surprise party. One of their moms offered to postpone it, but I begged her to stick with the plan. For whatever reason, Jensyn often got sick on special family days; we had been in the hospital three out of Tygen's last four birthdays! Missing his birthday was a big deal, but missing his sixteenth birthday felt even more significant. I texted Tygen in the morning to tell him how sorry I was to miss this day.

September 30, 2020

Me: I hate that I am away today! We were going to have so much fun doing school on your big day! Ha!

Tygen: It's okay. Don't worry about me. It's just another day.

Me: It is NOT just another day! It is my most responsible, adorable, hilarious son's 16th birthday. THAT is a BIG DEAL!!

Tygen: Okay, but so is keeping that son's baby sister alive, so focus on that, please.

Me. I will. But I can still be bummed I am missing your day.

Although I was grateful that Tygen understood the severity of Jensyn's needs and that I was where I should be, it was not easy to miss his special day. The girls managed to pull off the surprise, and my friend, Katrina, Facetimed me so that I could see his reaction and "party" with them somehow.

Shortly after being intubated, we learned that Jensyn was brewing a UTI and had tested positive for the rhinovirus (a common cold for typical people). She went from zero to crazy sick so quickly. The intubation allowed her to rest to some extent, but she would get agitated so quickly whenever the respiratory therapist (RT) came in to do a breathing treatment. She would desat (drop her oxygen) so low that they would need to use the Ambu bag to get her breathing to stabilize. It was brutal to watch her struggle. There were times when her oxygen saturation would drop into the teens and twenties—she was noticeably struggling.

I rarely feared Jensyn getting so sick she could not rebound from it. However, this time, I wrote about my feelings in her journal.

October 1, 2020

Oh, Sweet Jensyn! This has not been an easy hospital stay! I hate that you have to be here and that you are so sick. You were fine a few days ago, and now you are fighting for your life. It just doesn't seem fair!

When I left you last night to go to my sleep room, you had just had one of your desat episodes, but you were settled before I left. It was okay, but then around midnight, when I was trying to fall asleep, I could not settle myself! I had such a pit in my gut and could not articulate why! It felt like an elephant was camped out on my chest. I was just so sad and concerned. I had to wonder what had me so unsettled and anxious. I don't usually get super anxious, so this concerned me. I had no choice but to turn on some worship music and have a good cry. I know God loves you more than I do, but I am not ready for anything to happen to you—I just cannot stomach the thought of it. I was awake for a while longer, but then I felt at peace to sleep.

It was so great to see you and to touch you this morning. You seem to be doing better today, and you still have fight left in you.

Dad is coming to stay with you tonight so I can go home and better prepare to stay here long-term with you. It will NOT be easy to leave you today, but I feel better knowing you have had a more settled day.

I will hurry back! Keep fighting hard because next time,
I want to take you home with me. Whatever it takes . . .

I love you so!
Mom

It became clear this would not be a quick hospital stay. Because of the coronavirus, only Chris and I could be at the hospital with Jensyn, so I knew I needed to go home to get whatever I needed since I could not have people bring me stuff as they had in the past.

Sometimes, Chris would make an entry in Jensyn's journal. Clearly, he agreed that Jensyn was struggling more than we had ever seen her struggle. He also witnessed a few of her desat episodes and agreed they were triggering and hard to watch. His journal entry is so raw and real as he reflected on Jensyn at this time.

October 3, 2020

The past few days have been some of the toughest we
have faced with you, Jensyn. The ambulance leaving
our house with the lights and sirens on right away
should have been a clue—probably WAS the clue—that
this was serious. But you've been so well, and you're
stronger, so there was no reason to be overly concerned.
Until Mom texted me that you needed to be intubated

upon arrival. I made my way down to the hospital to be with Mom and make sure you were okay. I told the kids Mom needed her laptop because I didn't want them to be too concerned.

This afternoon, when the RT came in to do one of your treatments, I witnessed one of your episodes. Alarms started beeping, and you, in your sedated state, were moving in discomfort. Then I saw your eyes roll up in your head, your O2 sats dipped into the single digits, and your lips turned blue as the RT, nurse, and doctor quickly (but somehow calmly) worked the Ambubag. They were able to get your sats up to 45 percent, but the bag had a faulty valve, and pretty soon, you dove back into the single digits.

Thankfully, I knew screaming wouldn't do any good, but inside, I was thrashing with concern, so much so that I knew if I didn't sit down, I would soon be on the floor, and they'd need to call in more help. At this point, five people were working on you.

So, I took a seat and reminded myself of some things I reflected on while driving down here yesterday:

1. *Worrying isn't going to change a thing for you.*
2. *God can be trusted.*

3. *He'll do what will result in the greatest glory to His name.*

4. *He is always working for our good and His glory.*

5. *Hundreds of people are praying for you—they love you and our family!*

It would be devastating to lose you, Jensyn! People may look at you and wonder what difference you make, but we know the difference can only be measured in faith and character—just look at your siblings and our support system! You ARE making a difference!

I love you,
Dad

It was obvious to both Chris and me that things seemed different for Jensyn this time. Both of us were worried and unsure. This was new territory, and we had to dig a little deeper to trust God's plan.

After being intubated for about a week, Jensyn seemed to be waking up a bit. Doctors anticipated getting the breathing tube out, and after eight days, it was go time. Chris was planning to come after lunch to be with us for the extubation. Jensyn decided she was ready sooner than originally planned, so the doctor and the rest of her team decided to proceed. Initially, she did okay, but within the first hour after the tube came out, she was not in a good place. The team was doing all they could to keep her secretions under control, but she was not keeping her oxygen saturation high enough. Just as I was receiving the news that the doctor felt we needed to put the breathing tube back in, Chris arrived.

We agreed that she did not seem strong enough on her own and moved aside so that they could prepare for the new intubation. As they scrambled to get everything ready, Jensyn was able to rest from all of the intervention. We heard them say that all was ready, and we assumed it was time for the tube. Just as the doctor was ready to re-insert the tube, she told everyone to pause. We heard her say that she knew what she was about to say would not make sense, but she said that during the commotion of getting ready for the procedure, Jensyn had calmed and was recruiting enough air in her lungs to keep her saturation higher. She went on to say that Jensyn's lungs seemed clearer at that moment than they had been right after taking out the tube. Dr. Patel told the team she had changed her mind, and she believed it was worth it to give Jensyn more time to prove herself and to see if she could avoid tube replacement.

Jensyn did avoid getting the tube replaced. She was on a crazy high amount of oxygen and full BiPap, but she was proving once again to be the fighter that we knew she was! This was also evidence of the power of the prayer that covered her! As soon as the extubation was in the plans, I had sent word out to our warriors. Prayers were going up all over for a successful extubation. Once I saw she was struggling, I asked for prayer once again. Admittedly defeated, I shared the news that it was a "no-go" and that they were preparing to reinsert the tube. When I heard the doctor's surprised voice say that she wanted to pause the intubation, I knew the Lord was with us in that hospital room. I absolutely believe that God chose to answer the prayers on Jensyn's behalf, and He did it so this team of medical personnel and all of us would see He is ultimately in control.

GOD.
HE SHOWED UP.
HE SHOWED OFF.

I had watched Jensyn struggle horribly for over an hour. I was at the point of wanting them to make the suffering stop, even if that meant re-intubating her. I honestly felt defeated. After the crazy settled and Jensyn began to rest, I took a moment to see the situation for what it really was: God. He had answered prayer. He had sustained Jensyn. He had given wisdom to our young doctor. He showed up. He showed off. And we gave Him the glory for this great thing He had done.

Watching God at work in Jensyn was always a treat, yet it was hard to understand at the same time. It did not seem fair, in a way, that God would use Jensyn's life to teach all of us, to wake up insecurities and strengthen the faith in our lives. Because we believed that our lives are meant to be lived to bring glory to God, we wanted God to use us to reflect His love to others. Jensyn's life did this so well. She endured so much, yet she still had so much to give. Being her mom and fighting the daily battles alongside her was a gift.

Jensyn had become so well known at the hospital that most of the medical staff knew she did not always respond to treatments and therapies the way a typical child would respond. Pretty early on, one of her doctors coined the phrase "Jensyn Time" to describe how slowly or quickly she would progress or recover. This hospital stay gave a whole new meaning to "Jensyn Time." Slow and erratic—she did not indicate when she would turn a corner and feel better. In fact, after being in the hospital for thirteen days and off the breathing tube for five, I had the conversation with her doctor that no parent ever wants to have.

Each morning in the PICU, the medical team does rounds to figure out the plan of attack for the day. Parents are invited to attend the rounds to add their thoughts or ask questions. It was a Sunday morning, and I was by myself with Jensyn. Dr. Brockman went over things with Jensyn's team and said he would come by after rounds to check in with me and review some things. I did not see any issue with this, so I agreed to see him later. This doctor was familiar to us and had previously cared for Jensyn and our family.

When the doctor returned to our room, I was sitting on the couch writing lesson plans for the week ahead. He asked if he could pull up a chair; I was fine with that. We made small talk for a minute—he asked what I was doing, and we discussed homeschooling and the classes I was teaching. He then asked me how I thought things were going for Jensyn. Not realizing what he was indicating, I replied that she was on Jensyn Time and that I believed she would eventually pull it together. It soon became apparent that he felt much differently about things. He told me that if Jensyn did not get stronger, they would have to put the breathing tube back in. Then he told me he did not believe that was the right decision and that multiple intubations are not a good idea for someone like Jensyn. As he shared his "concerns," I began to cry.

"Do you have children?" I asked.

"Not yet," he said. "We are having our first child in January."

"If this was your child, what would you do?" I questioned.

Slowly, deliberately, he responded that if he were in my position, he would let his child go, that it would be more selfish to keep her with us than to give her up. I. Was. Devastated. And I knew then that I never wanted to have another conversation like this without Chris present. To have to call him and reiterate all that we had discussed was beyond brutal, and I could hardly talk through my sobs and tears. I knew that I needed Chris to come be with us, and I asked the doctor to come back the next day when Chris was there so that he could hear the doctor's heart and ask his questions regarding expectations and projections.

The next day, true to his word, Dr. Brockman returned to meet with Chris and me. Earlier that morning, the pulmonologist had given us a bit of false hope by saying that her lungs were sounding clearer and that they did not feel things were necessarily getting worse. However, by the time we met with the doctor, we had all begun to see a marked decline in Jensyn's fight and energy. She was weakening before our very eyes. Chris asked all of his questions, the biggest being how we could ensure that all her siblings could see her and if it might be time for Maci to fly home from Mexico.

The doctor believed Jensyn's hours were limited, so we called Maci to see what she wanted to do. Within a very short time and with some help from her friends at

YWAM, Maci was on a flight home. It was 4:00 p.m., and her flight was supposed to land at 11:45 p.m. Originally, we discussed how deeply important it was for the rest of our kids to be able to see Jensyn if the doctor really felt her life could be ending. He said they would do whatever they could to help us get her home, even if it meant he would escort her himself in the ambulance. He was very clear that if Jensyn continued to decline, the only thing they could do for her was re-intubate her, but his heartfelt advice was that he did not think it would work for her and that it was not the best decision.

The doctor who came on for the night shift said she agreed with that opinion and that we should "begin to think about what was best for Jensyn." Again, we mentioned that our other kids needed to be able to see her. She then informed us that the charge nurse had just lifted the visitor ban for our family. Anyone we felt needed to say goodbye to Jensyn could now come to the hospital.

We were heartbroken and uncertain and had no peace about anything except figuring out how to get people there to see Jensyn. Max and Sidney were the first to come, and we also extended the invitation to her nurse, Denice. Before Denice came, Chris and I were so unsettled that we were texting her about what the doctors were saying. At one point, she texted that she believed Chris and I knew the right thing to do but that we were second-guessing ourselves because the medical community's voice was so loud. She said, "I feel you know in your hearts what to do, but you're afraid to do it because you've been told it won't work. So you try it, and if it works, it does, right? And if it doesn't, you know it is her time to be with Jesus."

Max, Sidney, and Denice made it to the hospital and could quickly see what Chris and I had been observing for several hours. Jensyn was weak. Jensyn was tired. Jensyn was struggling. Jensyn needed rescuing, and we were the ones to figure out how to best save her. Chris and I were still not convinced we should not intubate her. It felt to us that we were giving up. It felt that by not giving her at least the chance to rest and recover, we were saying that she was done; that we were done. There was no peace in that. Knowing Maci was on her way and that the other kids still needed to see her, we decided that putting the tube in would buy us time, even if it prolonged the inevitable.

The doctor told us that with Jensyn needing 100 percent oxygen, there really was no way they could intubate her. We needed her to go down on her oxygen support so that she would have some reserve, giving them some wiggle room to get the tube in. At one point, she was able to be at 90 percent, so we called in the doctor and told her we wanted her to put the tube back in.

This time, the team asked us to wait in a room next door. As soon as we got word that Maci's plane had landed, we sent Max and Sid to pick her up. We waited with Denice to get word on the intubation. The wait was torture. The worry was intense. About fifty minutes later, Jensyn's nurse reported that the tube had gone in easily, but they had not been able to keep her oxygen high enough to stabilize her. We could only hope Maci would make it in time.

We were still waiting in the other room when Max and Sidney returned with Maci. Several minutes later, the doctor came to tell us that she was holding on but that it was not looking like a good hold. They allowed us to go back into Jensyn's room, and the reunion between Maci and her Jensyn is one I will never forget. She crawled into bed with her sister, prayed over her, and played the song God had given her when Jensyn was born. So many tears of anguish, uncertainty, and pleading with the Lord for her life.

At this point, Jensyn's oxygen was hanging out in the 80s. We needed it to get back up into the 90s. Once again, we asked the hard question: will it be too late if we wait until morning for her siblings to come? Jensyn's team declared that they could not promise the news we were hoping for, so Denice drove the hour and a half back to Becker to pick up my mom and the kids so they could come to see Jensyn. I still cannot imagine what went through the kids' minds when my mom woke them up at 2:00 a.m. to get in the van to see their sister. But we were reunited as a complete family at 3:30 a.m., and that is something I will never forget. Earlier, we had told the kids that Maci was coming home and that things were rocky with Jens, so even though they knew, it was still a tough night for them. The hospital was super accommodating; they even opened up sleep rooms for our entire family so we could be together, no matter what happened.

Jensyn made it through the night and began relaxing on the vent. Chris's parents and his brother, Tim, visited Jensyn the next day. As I was getting ready to go to Jensyn's room, I was in the middle of yet another good cry. There was so much crying. It was in that moment that God reminded me that when visitors were NOT allowed in hospital settings, we had just been given the insane gift of having our entire family together. If the intubation failed and if Jensyn's days were nearing the end, there would be plenty of time for crying and sadness. But this day needed to be about celebrating our time together. My entire family—even Maci, home from Mexico—was together in a hospital during the pandemic, supporting each other. For us to miss the blessing in all of this felt like a loss too great to bear.

We spent time cuddling Jensyn, kissing Jensyn, praying over Jensyn, and sometimes crying for Jensyn, but we were together with Jensyn. Earlier that morning, I was alone in Jensyn's room when Dr. Brockman came to see us. When he had left the day before, I think he believed

"YOU DO KNOW, HOWEVER, THERE WILL COME A DAY WHEN YOU WILL LEAVE THIS HOSPITAL WITHOUT HER." we would take his advice not to re-intubate her. Of course, it was clear that we had not.

I looked at him and said, "We had to buy some time, Doctor. We had to do it even if we have just prolonged the inevitable." I will never forget what he said.

"I understand that, and I think you made the right decision."

Yet, what he said next still haunts me to this day. "You do know, however, there will come a day when you will leave this hospital without her."

Those words! I heard them, I stored them, and I have never forgotten them. Sometimes, there is more comfort in things being left unsaid, and I am not sure what he was hoping to accomplish by telling me that, but I was confident that *this* time would not be *that* time. I had every intention of taking my girl home!

As the day went on, we were excited for the small victories Jensyn had—decreased oxygen needs and good, good rest. The family eventually went home, and Chris and I were once again alone with our girl. She seemed exhausted and worn out, and the mood was still sad and uncertain. Our hearts were anxious about what might still be, but we also had moments of knowing that had we followed the advice of two doctors, our daughter would not still be with us. By reinserting the tube, we had bought enough time to have a day together with our family, and by making the decision we did, we could live without regret.

We went to bed that night exhausted and with heavy, heavy hearts. How does a family prepare for something of this magnitude? Of possibly losing a loved one, a child who has been such a huge part of life? We talked about how much we loved our girl and how it was a privilege to be her parents. We discussed how proud we were of our other kids and how they allowed Jensyn to be used in their lives to grow their faith. We cried. We prayed. We tried to rest. And we hoped for a better day.

When we got to Jensyn's room the next day, we saw a very different little girl. Jensyn's oxygen needs were at 30 percent, and her saturation was in the 90s. The doctor said that her lung X-rays had cleared up immensely and that the difference between her lungs from a few days prior was unbelievable. The doctor who had those difficult conversations with us earlier in the week said that Jensyn was "exceeding his expectations." I guess it is good that God's expectations are higher than anything we can even imagine.

Jensyn remained intubated for another five days. During that time, palliative care and a new doctor came to have another meeting with Chris and me. Their goal was to prepare us for extubation and to talk to us about updating Jensyn's POLST (Physicians Orders for Life-Sustaining Treatment). Again, the palliative care doctor shared that allowing Jensyn to "go" showed Jensyn great love and selflessness. They often questioned Jensyn's quality of life and wondered if continuing to intervene with her health issues to keep her with us was fair to her. We never questioned her quality of life. The joy she brought to our family and the lessons she taught us each day not only made her life worth living but also made her an integral part of our family. We believed it was more selfless to serve her and care for her than it ever was to "let her go."

As for the POLST, at this point, we had always listed Jensyn as "full code." This meant that no matter what, Jensyn would be given any and all life-sustaining treatments. The doctor who met with us that day asked us to rethink things. She believed that if this extubation failed, it would not be in anyone's best interest to intubate again. We agreed. Also, she suggested that resuscitating her would be more harmful than beneficial. Again, we agreed that she could rewrite the directives, but only for that hospital stay. We wanted her to return to full code when we made it out of there.

This next extubation was night and day different from the previous one. Jensyn rode the roller coaster of ups and downs for a few days, but then she stabilized and began the upward trek of getting stronger. We had another scare shortly after the extubation when we had our kids return to the hospital, but it was short-lived, and we soon had the assurance that we would eventually be able to take Jensyn home.

Forty days! After forty days in the PICU, Jensyn was finally well enough to be discharged. The shock of all that had happened in those forty days stayed with our family long after we finally made it home. As I remember that time in the hospital, I recall devastation. I remember dependence, and I was so grateful for deliverance. God allowed us more time with Jensyn, and we saw that as the glorious gift it was. When Jensyn was born, God gave Maci a song for her called "You're Not Finished Yet" by The Belonging Co. As Jensyn and I were getting ready to leave the hospital after those forty days, I played that song. The lyrics reminded me that God's plans for Jensyn's life were not finished yet and that God was in the process of healing two of my girls who had experienced real trauma in that fall of 2020. As I held Jensyn and listened to that song, I wondered if maybe God had allowed this to happen so that Maci would come home. And maybe God knew that, ultimately, Jensyn and Maci needed each other to heal. Perhaps what I wrote on Jensyn's CaringBridge the morning of Day 40 says it best:

November 6, 2020

*So, Day 40—we get to go home! And what a
homecoming it will be! I know some very excited
siblings have wondered if this day would ever happen.
We cannot wait to be reunited. I wish this could be a
season that we could proverbially wrap up in a shiny
bow and cut off the loose, frazzled ends, but sadly,
Jensyn will still struggle. We will continue to social
distance for her and do all we can to meet her every
need. We are taking her home with her respiratory
being better than it has been in a long time—how is
that even possible after two intubations? And although
respiratory is amazing and miraculous, her current
struggles are neurological in nature. This morning, she
was fussy—Jensyn is rarely fussy—and when I figured
out that the cure for the crabbies was Mama holding
Daughter, it dawned on me. She absolutely needs the
love and touch of her family to finish this. I told the
doctors that as long as she could breathe, we could
handle the rest.*

*I am leaving here today armed with the meds she
needs, the memories of amazing doctors and nurses
who truly love my girl, and the motivation to love her
back to strength. Of course, if you are still willing to
pray, we will also take that. The t-shirt I am wearing*

today says this: "Trisomy 5p does not come with a manual; it comes with a mother that never gives up." I love it and wear it with pride, but it has a typo. "Mother" should say "a whole bunch of people" because this was a team effort, and it took everybody to win.

Nobody will ever forget 2020, and even though parts of it were extremely difficult for our family, we will also remember the good that came because of it. Maci survived her apartment explosion and Jensyn beat death. Truly, we could have been planning two funerals within those three months, but instead, both girls were home together, healing and getting stronger. And in December, their first nephew, my first grandbaby, Crosby Christopher, was born. Suddenly, after the hardest of hards, we had so much to celebrate!

COVID-19 AND SCOLIOSIS

After a crazy 2020, we hoped for a better year ahead. At age four, Jensyn became an aunt for the first time, having already lived a pretty full life. Although she could not physically hold Crosby, she loved it when we placed him by her in bed or in her P-Pod chair for a quick cuddle.

The beginning of 2021 brought with it the hope that our family could finally slow down, but that hope was dashed when the family succumbed to the coronavirus. Six of the nine got it simultaneously—only Jakely, Jensyn, and I were still going strong. After what we had gone through with Jensyn the previous fall, we decided to have the sick ones quarantine in the basement while I tended to them and Jensyn. Jakely was next to get it about two days into the quarantine, so she joined the others banished to the basement. This left me to cook, clean, shuttle food downstairs, and collect dirty dishes back upstairs on top of caring for Jensyn. I was exhausted and frustrated. Even though they were sick, my entire family was downstairs watching movies and playing games (the kids were not sick for long) while I tended to their every need. In Chris's defense, he got hit pretty hard, so I am not sure he was too thrilled with being Dad in the midst of it all.

About a week into the quarantine, it was my turn to get sick. Since I had been with Jensyn the most, it did not make sense for anyone else to take over her care. Now, not only did I have to tend to the crew downstairs, but I also had to glove up, mask up, and cover up to meet Jensyn's needs upstairs. We were blessed that Denice was willing to subject herself to our sick house to help me with Jensyn when she could. Jensyn's pulmonologist was concerned enough for Jensyn that she suggested I take her to Children's to get the convalescent plasma infusion, which was seen as a preventative measure against the virus. I remember thinking I had no business being at the hospital as I was already feeling pretty rough, but we knew that we would do whatever it took to ensure she stayed as healthy and strong as possible. The hospital knew I had tested positive for COVID-19, but they were still willing to let me come—another weird inconsistency that I was grateful for.

Once we rebounded from the virus (Jensyn never got COVID-19 then or ever), we were again hopeful things would level out and we would get a chance to catch our breath. A new year meant more new changes in our home for Jensyn. When we first moved to the new house, Jensyn was in our room. Next, she moved down the hall to a room she shared with Brinkley. Eventually, her equipment needs were too many and her machines too loud, so Brinkley graciously relocated. Although having her on the same floor as Chris and me was helpful and comforting, it was getting harder and more laborious to haul her machines and equipment downstairs every morning and upstairs every evening. We knew it was time to figure out a room for her on the main floor. She was also not getting any smaller, so carrying her upstairs multiple times a day was taxing on all her caregivers. She spent most of the day lying out in the living room since she needed to be near us, and this became risky if we had people over or if someone in the family was sick. She needed her own space so she could quarantine and rest when necessary.

Since there was no bedroom on the main floor, we decided to modify the office to create a room for Jensyn. As part of her new waiver that year, we were able to have someone custom-make shelves and cubbies for all of her machines so they could be stored while still being available for use throughout the day. Sidney, Maci, and I created a special room for her with lots of visual interest, as we knew she would be spending a lot of time in her room. Jensyn had always been a good sleeper, and the older she got, the more she seemed to find comfort in napping. Early on, we dubbed her our Sleepy Sloth. Around that time, sloths seemed to be on trend, so it was easy to start a collection. Because she loved sloths, we felt Boho colors and a jungle theme fit her best. She even had a massive sloth—given to her by her Make-A-Wish granters, Ashley and Karen—hanging from her ceiling. Each sloth had a name, and each became part of her story: like a sloth, Jensyn tended to be sleepy, slow, compassionate, and quiet yet absolutely cuddly and loveable at the same time.

Creating space for Jensyn on the main floor was a welcome change to the rhythms of our home. It was nice to have her near us at all times during the day, and she was only a flight of stairs away if she needed us in the middle of the night. The daybed we put in her room allowed Denice to do overnights, which was a huge help as Jensyn got older and her needs increased. This gave both Jensyn and Denice their own space and offered the rest of the family a chance to have their own areas as well.

Grateful that Jensyn had avoided the coronavirus and seemed to be gaining some strength, we began the process of meeting with a spine doctor. Jensyn's spine had never been straight. She had undergone a lot of physical therapy to help her strengthen her core and figure out some head control, but she was fighting a losing battle as her spine continued to curve. We met with the spine doctor several times, and he recommended doing the MAGEC rod surgery to straighten her back.

MAGEC rods treat certain types of scoliosis. MAGEC stands for MAGnetic Expansion Control. Unlike rod surgeries of the past, where rods were placed surgically and then surgically lengthened as the child grew, these rods are placed surgically at first, but they can be lengthened in the clinic using a remote control and powerful magnets. This eliminates the need for numerous surgeries while accomplishing the same thing. Of course, we had to meet with a team of people before this big surgery, and there was some question about whether putting Jensyn through the surgery would be worth it. We believed it would give her a better quality of life. Her new pulmonologist, Dr. Mikesell, agreed that straightening the spine could help her respiratory system operate better. Physical therapists believed this could help her body relax and move better, and her neurologist was all for it. He reiterated that if it gave her a better quality of life, it would be a good thing. Only palliative gave us pause. "Just because we can do something doesn't mean we should," they said. We chose to ignore that one voice and agree with the rest.

In September 2021, after only being hospitalized a handful of times for minor UTIs or respiratory junk in the months before, we admitted Jensyn for spine surgery. This time, she was at Gillette Children's Hospital because that is where Dr. Perra was, and we believed he was the best one to do the surgery. Although they did not know Jensyn like the other two children's hospitals did, it did not take them long to fall prey to her sweet charm and unpredictability. The surgery went as planned, but they soon learned about Jensyn Time when they tried to stabilize her enough to get her extubated after the surgery. They tried to do things the usual way, but it didn't work, so they put the tube back in. Although the process was a bit scary after what we had gone through the year before, she rebounded the next day, started breathing independently, and rocked her new rods.

Recovery was pretty quick, and the results were evident as well. She remained on oxygen, but her work of breathing was less, and we were hopeful that we would see fewer issues with respiratory. Aside from a quick emergency room visit in October, Jensyn spent no more time in the hospital in 2021. When we reflected on almost losing her the year before, we chose to celebrate the uneventful year with which we had been blessed. And much like the end of 2020 being a time for celebration, the end of 2021 was also a special time. Jensyn was going to have a new brother-in-law. While Maci was home in January 2021, healing from her fire trauma and the scare of almost losing Jensyn, she decided to visit some Tennessee friends she had met the summer before in Mexico. This was when she met Chase. At the end of

2021, Chase proposed to Maci, and we had a new goal for Jensyn. She had a critical job to do in July 2022, and there was absolutely no way Maci could get married without Jensyn being part of her day.

We were so grateful for 2021. It was a good year. It was a year to calm the crazy and the chaos of 2020 and a time to grow as a family as we did what we could to rest and restore. Unfortunately, we had mastered living in survival mode, which meant things never stayed chill for long.

FULL CODE

Jensyn became an aunt again in January 2022. Max and Sidney gave birth to our first granddaughter a month after Crosby turned one. Sadie Elise was a sweet addition to our family. Sidney continued to work with Jensyn five days a week, so it was always a take-your-kids-to-work day for her. This grandma did not mind! I loved seeing my grandkids almost daily, and although it often made homeschooling a little more hectic, the aunts and uncles had no complaints either. I was grateful that Sidney was still willing to work with Jensyn, and we have many fond memories of taking Jensyn to appointments with one or both of the grandkids tagging along as well.

Having a lot of people in our home became the norm. Sidney and the grandkids came every weekday, sometimes Max worked from home and would come for lunch one or two days a week, Lowell and Linda came twice a month to clean, Maci had moved home, and Denice came several days to work and sometimes did overnight shifts as well. Jensyn was not strong enough to do preschool at school, so her teachers and therapists came out three times a week. If someone was not coming to our house, we were taking Jensyn to appointments. Even though Jensyn's spine surgery helped strengthen her respiratory system, we began chasing UTIs. It did not matter what we did. She averaged one every five to six weeks, and I had her pediatrician and her urology nurses on speed dial. We were constantly taking in samples and trying new antibiotics and flushes to do what we could to stay ahead.

Unfortunately, when she got a UTI, the infection would affect her in other areas. She would get a fever, her blood pressure would be all over the place, and she just never seemed to feel very good. It was hard to watch, but we kept doing everything we could possibly do for her, hoping we would eventually find something that worked.

Jensyn was able to stay out of the hospital throughout the holidays and even through the winter months of 2022. Aside from the UTIs, it felt like we were having another great year, all things considered. My other kids were enduring some medical stuff, so it was nice not to have Jensyn needing advanced medical care on top of it all. Maci had surgery in January, Tygen tore his meniscus in February during basketball and had to have it surgically repaired, Sidney had emergency gallbladder surgery in March, and Chris had his gallbladder out after Sidney. Things were all over the place with the rest of the family, but again, I was grateful Jensyn was doing okay. Until April.

It was a Friday night and also Max's birthday. Chris and I helped with a huge game night event for our church. Denice was with Jensyn because our adult kids were with us at the event. We got home late, and since Denice was there, we did not check on Jensyn and went straight to bed. Jensyn had a low-grade fever the Thursday morning before, so I had taken a urine sample to her pediatrician. The urine returned clean, so we were unsure what the fever indicated. She was not showing any other symptoms besides being more tired and lethargic than usual. Being so sleepy at baseline made it difficult to determine when she was actually more out of it than usual, so there was always concern that we might be missing something.

On Saturday, around 7:50 a.m., Denice called my cell phone and asked me to come downstairs. As soon as I joined her, she told me to call 911 because she suddenly had huge concerns about Jensyn. She was cold, she was lethargic, her blood pressure was low, and she was not responding well. We called 911, and I pulled some stuff together, but I barely had time to join them in the ambulance before we were lights and sirens out of our driveway. Once again, Jensyn had gone from sick to ridiculously sick in a matter of minutes.

Denice told the EMT she would join me in the ambulance, and he did not question her assistance. This time, we both sat in the back with the paramedic and helped with what we could. Denice and the EMT seemed to be having a silent conversation with their eyes, and from what I could tell, it had to do with Jensyn's blood pressure being crazy low—like 40 over nothing at one point. The fear was that she was becoming septic and going into shock. Though the vibe was tense and unsettling, I did not know how dire the situation was until the paramedic told me we needed to divert. He said we would not make it to St. Paul Children's and needed to go to North Memorial. I told him, "They don't know Jensyn. We have to go where they know her. Can we at least get to Minneapolis Children's?"

He agreed to go to Minneapolis, and then he did something a mama should never have to watch someone do to her child. He gave Jensyn an IO. Intraosseous (IO) vascular access is the placement of a specialized hollow-bore needle through the cortex of a bone and into the marrow. Essentially, it is a hole that allows fast administration of fluids and medications when ordinary methods (like IVs) do not suffice. The device looks like a drill. The fact that I had to watch him drill into Jensyn's tibia once was bad enough, but because the first time did not work, I had to watch him do it twice. It was barbaric and made me sick to my stomach. I had observed many scary things where Jensyn was concerned, but this was one of the most unsettling things I had ever seen.

THEY CONFIRMED SEPTIC SHOCK, AND ALL OF A SUDDEN, JENSYN WAS CRITICAL ONCE AGAIN.

Although this was not the first time we had a full team of people waiting for us upon arrival, it was far more upsetting this time. That "full code" we had asked to be reinstated for her POLST was now being enacted before my eyes. Sixteen medical personnel tended to Jensyn while I stood back and watched. It was traumatizing, but since we had been in this position before, I did what I could to remain calm—on the outside. When they cut off her sweatshirt and crashed her bed, pushing me into the back corners of the trauma room by the force of their presence and activity alone, I knew that my calm might crack at any moment.

They confirmed septic shock, and all of a sudden, Jensyn was critical once again. Jensyn's blood pressure was still not coming up, her breathing was getting weaker, and the crew was unsure of what else to do. We agreed to intubation, and after one miserable, failed attempt, they managed to get the tube in. While all of this was going on, they pumped her with fluids to get her blood pressure back up. When they stabilized her enough in the ED for us to move to the PICU, I finally got the chance to see my girl. She looked puffed up, bloated, and not at all like my skinny sweet daughter. My calm was beginning to collapse, and the tears began to fall. Once again, I was left asking: How could things have gotten so bad so quickly?

Typically, we follow the bed up to the room and file in. This time, they sent us to a family waiting room so they could get her settled. It seemed a bit odd to me, but I complied. It took so long for them to get her situated that Chris joined Denice and me within that time. The intensivist came to chat with us, and he did not have good news. He agreed that she was septic and that intubating her was the right decision. Due to the size of her abdomen, he believed something was very wrong with her belly. He said we needed to be aware that everything happening to her was life-threatening. Again, how had she gotten so sick so quickly? My calm continued to crumble. More tears. More questions. More waiting.

The doctor returned to the room to work on Jensyn, and we sent prayer requests to as many people as possible. He came back a bit later to say they had put in a Foley catheter (a tube that drains the bladder) and that it had done a lot to release the bloating and the pressure in her tummy. They had given her so much fluid in the ED, and since she is not great at emptying her bladder, she had gotten very full. Once she voided the extra, things began to slow down enough to allow her to stabilize.

They ordered a CT scan of her abdomen, which showed some insane inflammation in her intestines and colon. This was extremely serious for someone like Jensyn. They said that if the antibiotics did not help this inflammation, they could not do much more to help her. My calm kept crumbling.

Chris and I remained with Jensyn through the night. She was stable and doing pretty well. As we looked over our daughter the next morning, she seemed at peace. She still looked extremely puffy and swollen, and she was still hooked up to more than a dozen IV drips and had even had a blood transfusion. She did not lose a lot of blood, but they were taking an insane amount of blood trying to figure out why she had become so sick.

When the doctor came in that morning, she said she could not believe she was looking at the same child who had come in the day before. They could not figure out the culprit for the inflammation all over her body and were unable to find the source of the infection. Her urine was clear, her blood was not growing anything, and none of the tests returned with answers. But Jensyn was better—markedly better—and nobody who had seen her the day before could figure out why. Once again, we attributed it to prayer and God working on Jensyn's behalf.

When a child is brought to the hospital under full code, the intensivist is called to the ED to assist the doctors there. Dr. Flynn was the doctor who had put in Jensyn's breathing tube and was now answering our questions. Chris asked her if Jensyn's blood pressure had actually gotten as low as 40 over almost nothing, and if so, what that meant. She said that Jensyn was minutes away from needing CPR (cardiopulmonary resuscitation). This prompted me to ask if Jensyn would have made it if we had not diverted to Minneapolis. She said, "You did the right thing by getting here when you did." So, if she had been so critical that we almost lost her upon arrival (her full code lasted an hour and a half), we were told when we got to the floor that her swollen abdomen was life-threatening, and then the surgeon told us that the inflammation in her bowels could require surgery that could be fatal for someone like Jensyn, only to be told the next day that she looked like a completely different child—how could we not agree that God had performed a miracle? Jensyn was a fighter. Jensyn was an amazing little girl. But only with God could she have rebounded to this extent so quickly. So many blessings came with being Jensyn's mom, but how God used her life to show Himself to others was my favorite. Jesus and Jensyn always had a special connection.

While Chris and I were processing all of what was going on, he received a text from Tate.

"Hey, Dad, God's been telling me that we should read the Gospel to Jensyn. I would do it if she was here, but I think she needs to hear about the One who designed her. So, if you could do that, I think it would mean the world to her."

Yes, Tate. Even though I believe Jensyn did know the One who so intricately designed a body that in this world was broken but still had a sweet soul that changed lives, I do not think she ever got tired of hearing about Him. So, I decided to start with the Gospel of Matthew and vowed to read it to her until we received our discharge papers. I could not think of anything more worthwhile to refresh the calm that was still disintegrating in my life than to read the Word of God to my daughter. So that is what I did.

A couple of days later, we found ourselves in a holding pattern. Chris and I had individually done some research on septic shock. We both learned that the mortality rate is quite high when kids get to the state Jensyn was in. We learned she could have long-term problems because of what she had endured. We learned this often does happen very quickly. Before this, we had no idea. Once Chris and I processed all our findings together, we asked better questions, and it humbled us to realize that a child as medically fragile as Jensyn had beaten the fatality odds. Doctors continued to marvel at the crazy improvements Jensyn was making. There seemed to be an underlying astonishment that she was trending in the right direction. Because of the inflammation and sepsis, this hospital stay garnered a new specialist for Jensyn: an infectious disease doctor. We were hopeful this doctor would be able to help us with the new issues we were facing with Jensyn's health.

After eight days, Jensyn was still intubated. Even though they had mentioned extubation earlier in our stay, the pulmonologist wanted to give her body more time to rest and recover before possibly making it work harder. Again, we were on Jensyn Time. We understood Jensyn Time and were comfortable enough to let her call the shots.

I continued to read the Gospel to Jensyn. One night, I asked Jensyn's nurse if kids in comas could remember anything when they woke up and how much they could hear. She said they don't remember much, and she was unsure how much they could hear or process. I read to Jensyn every night before we went to bed. We were still reading out of Matthew, and I finished the night reading from Matthew 6:34: "Therefore, do not worry about tomorrow, for tomorrow will worry about itself. Each day has enough trouble of its own." I then cuddled her sweet head and prayed for her night. When I went to kiss her forehead, I noticed a tear coming out of her eye. As I wiped it away, it was then that I knew: my girl had heard the Word and had given me a moment I will never forget.

There were so many sacred moments in those hospital rooms, memories that are forever seared into my heart. Jensyn was eventually extubated, and even though her breathing was not the most significant issue this time, she still had more healing to do. We were in the hospital for twenty-six days altogether. It was long enough to miss Easter with the family, and I was not able to fly with Maci to Tennessee for her bridal shower with Chase's family and friends. It was always hard to have to miss these special things, but it had become somewhat normal at the same time. Ironically, since Maci's flight was super early in the morning and since the hospital was closer to the airport than home, she stayed with me at the hospital and I saved Chris a trek to the airport. Even in the hard, we found ways to make unique memories.

Another memory from this same hospital stay also includes Maci. After we were there for a week, Maci came to visit us and brought some stuff from home. Chris's fiftieth birthday was a few days away, and I had not had time to plan or purchase anything for his big day. My friend, Meghann, had just gotten a dog—a Bernedoodle—and his brother was still available for purchase. I have never wanted a dog and vowed I would never ever get one. But sleep deprivation, guilt for having no gift, and a very persuasive daughter proved to be the perfect storm for making the decision to gift Chris a dog. The kids named him after Jensyn's beloved stuffed puppy (a puppy who was famous at both hospitals—everyone knew Jensyn's favorite stuffy): Latte. I joke that once I agreed to the dog, I lost more sleep in the hospital about there being a dog in my house than I did worrying about my sick daughter! Though still not a dog lover, I am a fan of Latte. He is a great dog, and he has been a wonderful comfort to the family through the hard days without Jensyn.

After twenty-six days in the hospital, Jensyn was well enough to go home, even though she was not fully recovered. Her lungs were stronger, but the rest of her body had been through it. Unfortunately, we were only home a week before we headed back to the hospital. It was always difficult for me when the turnaround time was so quick, but at least this time, she was strong enough to make it to St. Paul.

FRACTURED

Once we got home, Jensyn remained weak and super sleepy, but we believed her to be doing well otherwise. The only new thing we noticed was some unexplained pain in her legs and hips. Whenever someone changed her diaper or tried to dress her, she whimpered and whined. It was so pitiful and heartbreaking. Sometimes, she would even start crying while just lying in her crib. We wondered if it was stiffness from being in the hospital for so long, but regardless, we knew we had to keep an eye on things. Even though her lungs were stronger, she was still recovering from respiratory stuff, and we were suctioning a lot, along with doing our best to keep up with breathing treatments throughout the day. Her oxygen levels were good, and she did not require extra oxygen, which was a win. Unfortunately, after being home for a little over a week, she woke up with a low-grade fever, which led us to believe she was brewing another UTI. She did not seem too sick at first, but we watched her closely.

Believing that we could continue to care for her at home, Denice came to stay with her, and Chris and I decided to take the family to a movie. After being away for so much of the month before, it was fun to be together. We ran errands and hit a graduation party after the movie. By the time we got home, it was obvious Jensyn had not fared as well as we had hoped. Her fever had exacerbated her oxygen need, and we noticed her struggling more with her respiratory. Once again, we knew it would be difficult to stay ahead of the crazy through the night, so we called for transport. No lights. No sirens—just a chill ride to St. Paul Children's. It was a nice reprieve from our previous ride the month before.

Upon arrival, we learned that Jensyn had pneumonia and that her lungs were aching for some help. Of course, the doctors soon saw that the rest of her body was an aching mess as well. Since Jensyn was not critical, she could be on a regular floor. We had not been on a regular floor since before 2020, and it felt like going home. Jensyn's "friends" from the fifth floor stopped to say hello, and we had the best team of students and doctors. Jensyn made an impression on people, and she was not easily forgotten. Even though I was grateful for the warm welcome and the friendly atmosphere, I hated that we were back in the hospital. I did not want to get in that ambulance. I did not want to leave the family again so soon after getting home. I did not want to see Jensyn suffer again. But we did what we had to do. The family had the memory of the precious time the day before of being together at the movie. And I believed we would go home sooner than later this time.

Five days later, we did get to go home. Unfortunately, we left again without answers. The pneumonia was under control, but the pain in her hips and legs was still a mystery. Maci and Chase's wedding was a little over two months away at the end of July, so we knew we needed to do what we could to keep Jensyn healthy and, if possible, figure out what was causing her so much discomfort.

We were so grateful to have made it through that lengthy hospital stay in April and that extra time in May. In June, Jensyn began pool therapy. The water had always been Jensyn's happy place, so much so that we chose a hot tub for Jensyn's Make-A-Wish (unfortunately, she never received her wish). Because COVID-19 protocol was still in place at Gillette's, where Jensyn did pool therapy, she needed someone to get in the water with her and the therapist. The therapist could guide and direct, but she could not touch or hold Jensyn. Tygen and Tate were more than willing to work with their sister, and Jensyn lit up whenever she could be in the pool. After several weeks, the therapist also noticed the pain and discomfort Jensyn often exhibited in her hips and legs. When Jensyn was discharged that May, she gained another specialist:

an orthopedic doctor. At an outpatient appointment, we learned that Jensyn had hip dysplasia. It was not severe enough to warrant surgery yet, so the plan was to keep her comfortable and do what we could to strengthen her by using her stander. We wondered if the hips were the cause of her pain.

Around this same time, we received word that Jensyn had been approved for a new stander. A stander is a piece of rehabilitation equipment that helps a child achieve sustained standing with supports and proper alignment while fully weight-bearing. Jensyn had grown enough to warrant getting a bigger, better stander, and we were thrilled for her. Insurance also approved a new wheelchair for Jensyn. Her previous "wheelchair" was something we called a glorified stroller, but her new wheels would be an actual wheelchair, formed and fitted to her.

When the technician came to the house to fit her for her stander, we put on her ankle braces and began the process of strapping her in. She tolerated her left side well, but when we put the brace on her right ankle, she screamed in pain. We had not always been as diligent with the braces as we should have been, so we figured she was just ticked that we were putting them on. However, the screaming continued when we moved to put her in the stander. Her scream was so unsettling that every person in the house came to see why she was in such distress.

It was heartbreaking to hear. We knew we needed to go back to her orthopedist.

After getting X-rays of her legs and hips, we found out that Jensyn had fractured her tibia. Our girl had a broken leg? How had we missed this? The fracture was tiny, and it was just below her knee where the EMT had drilled the IOs in her leg when she went septic in April. There was no clear indication that the two were connected, but we wondered just the same. Since Jensyn had such low bone density, they felt the leg could not support a cast. Instead, Jensyn wore a brace that covered her entire right leg for three weeks. Because of the brace, Jensyn's ankle muscles remained in a straightened position, and in order to get her ankle braces back on after her broken leg healed, we had to serial cast her ankle for six weeks. The biggest bummer for her was that she could no longer do pool therapy while wearing the brace or the casts, but in the midst of it all, she healed up nicely, just in time to be the most beautiful flower girl in Maci and Chase's wedding.

Jensyn got her shiny new wheelchair a week before the wedding, and Jakely proudly pushed her sister down the aisle. Jensyn looked gorgeous in her lacy flower girl dress that matched Maci's. Much like Max and Sidney's wedding, having Jensyn healthy and well enough to perform her role brought tears to the eyes of many. My heart was happy, but even more than that, Maci's dream of having Jensyn as part of her day was fulfilled. It meant so much, in fact, that when Jensyn was fighting for her life back in April, Maci had Chase on call to fly to Minnesota. If there had been even the slightest chance that Jensyn would not make it, Maci was prepared to tie the knot in Jensyn's hospital room. There was absolutely no way Maci was getting married without her Jensyn. Once again, God blessed our family by allowing us to celebrate another special day together!

EACH DAY, SHE RESPONDED TO US LESS AND LESS.

I believe there was a sense of denial when we looked at photos from the wedding day and from that summer. Many of the pictures showed Jensyn asleep in her wheelchair. Even in photos from the pool, she slept in her brother's arms. Each day, she responded to us less and less. Jensyn looked worn out and even somewhat sad most of the time. Of course, she had been through some rough stuff, yet we still believed we had the right team of specialists and the best crew of caregivers to help her build back her strength and stamina. However, seeing the evidence in the photos and knowing what her body had gone through in April and the residual damage it caused, we were having a harder time denying the toll it had taken on any fight she had left.

And it left us wondering if April might have been the beginning of the end.

INFECTED

Since birth, Jensyn fought a losing battle, and we had continued to observe a marked decline in the six years we cared for her. "It feels like we are just keeping her alive," Chris said once when we left her in the care of her siblings before heading to one of Tygen's basketball games in the fall of 2022. I hated to agree, but sadly, I had had those same thoughts and feelings as Jensyn seemed to grow weaker and weaker. Living in denial is a very real thing, yet we were willing to remain there. We had gotten pretty good at meeting her needs, and we had so many of the means necessary to keep her with us.

Unfortunately, 2022 only brought more struggles for her and, ultimately, for all of us. We could not stay ahead of her UTIs. They came more frequently, and though we tried antibiotic after antibiotic to fight the bugs, we feared she was becoming resistant to them.

Even though we made it through the summer, the fall proved to be a bit more frustrating as all falls seemed to be for Jensyn. After the issues with her broken leg and ankle casting, she seemed more fragile all the way around. Yet, Jensyn turned six in September, and it was time for kindergarten. Instead of going to kindergarten, kindergarten came to her. Her teacher, Miss Rachel was supposed to come each weekday for an hour to do school with Jensyn, but since Jensyn was such a sleepy sloth, we did what we could to determine the best time for her teachers and therapists.

Most days, she had a window of opportunity in the afternoon when she was a little more attentive and alert. However, schooling proved to be a struggle. That, coupled with the crazy amount of appointments we had each week, made it difficult for the teacher to come regularly. We were lucky if she was able to do school two days a week. Even though Miss Rachel did not get Jensyn's best effort and attention, their connection was still sweet, and having her in our lives was a joy. In fact, Jensyn's entire team from the school—Margaret, Lisa, Wendy, Joran, Kim, and Janene—impacted her life and ours in ways we will never forget. Watching people genuinely care about Jensyn when she could not give back was always a blessing to us.

Jensyn had a short hospital stay in October, which was a precursor to a longer one in November. UTIs continued to wreak havoc on her body. We knew we needed more intervention. The questions remained: did the UTIs cause the swelling and the erratic heart rates in her body because of infection, or was there more going on? In October, after just two days in the hospital, we assumed that the swelling and the crazy all-over-the-place heart rate were exacerbated by a yeast infection that was hanging out with another UTI. Fortunately, we were able to treat that and move on—sort of. Just a few weeks later, Jensyn was struggling—same saga, same villain.

We were beyond frustrated. After everything we had been through, we had gotten better at figuring out how to ward off some of the bad stuff before it happened. Seizures were stable. Respiratory was relatively relaxed. Neuro was nicely navigated. But these stinking UTIs! We could not figure out how to beat them. Miserable and mighty bacteria made for very difficult management, yet it was not for lack of trying.

At this point, we had learned to cath Jensyn ourselves—we did this three to five times a day for various reasons—and we had gotten adept at seeing the changes in her urine sooner, which was a blessing in her overall health. The bummer was that she could never fully heal from one infection before another was ready to pounce. In October, Candida yeast decided to join the party. This caused a new issue: swelling all over her body along with bradycardia, which is a low heart rate.

In November, she succumbed to the same—UTIs and wacky heart rates—and we found ourselves back in the hospital. At this point, they suggested that if we could not get these infections figured out, it might mean being in-patient every time she got a UTI so that she could have the big-gun IV antibiotics. Ain't nobody got time for that! The other option was to do a vesicostomy surgery. A vesicostomy is a surgical opening in the bladder to the outside of the lower belly that allows urine to drain, preventing urinary tract infections or damage to the kidneys. However, she could not have this surgery while she was in the middle of a UTI, which, at this point, seemed impossible.

Believing this would be a longer stay than the one in October, we hunkered down and waited for her infection to run its course. In typical Jensyn fashion, she picked another holiday hospital stay, and I prepared to miss Thanksgiving. Chase and Maci planned to go to Tennessee to see his family for the holiday, so we were going to celebrate early. Of course, they wanted to see Jensyn before leaving for the weekend, so they offered to bring Chris and me some lunch. When they got to Jensyn's room, Maci handed me our food. Famished, I reached into the bag. On top of my Chinese food was a red onesie. Confused by sleep deprivation, I wondered why this item of clothing was with my lunch. I picked it up and read the front: *Mas Amor, Por Favor.* It took a hot minute for things to register. "Shut up!" I said. "For real?" Jensyn was going to be an aunt AGAIN! As I have said before, we had so many special moments in those hospital rooms, and this was another indelible memory that I will always have with my oldest and youngest daughters.

Chase and Maci left for Tennessee; Jensyn and I stayed at the hospital. We missed Thanksgiving with the family, but the day before Thanksgiving, God showed up again. The IV antibiotics had worked their magic and got Jensyn in the right spot to have her vesicostomy surgery! There just happened to be a doctor available to do the surgery the day before a holiday, and the operating room miraculously had an opening in their schedule for her to get the procedure done. There were a lot of moving parts, and God moved them all.

The surgery went well, but after the surgery, Jensyn struggled to regulate. Fevers, wonky blood pressures, extra lethargy, and weird blood sugar levels added to the stress on her body. New doctors came on board, and cardiology was consulted for the first time since she was a baby. Things were in a tailspin while everyone tried to assess what was happening. The Sunday after Thanksgiving, Jensyn's nurse burst into the room and proclaimed that Jensyn needed to be prepped for imaging and ultrasounds. They also wanted to do an X-ray of her chest and ultrasounds of her liver, pancreas, spleen, kidneys, and abdomen. When I asked what exactly they were looking for, her nurse, Tracy, said that they wanted to see if her organs were still healthy or if there was an abscess or something they might be missing. What she said next sent my heart plummeting: "There is some concern that her organs might be shutting down." My response was to call Chris.

When we almost lost Jensyn in 2020, Chris was not with me when the doctor first delivered the horrific news that she might not make it. This new situation was another time I knew I needed Chris to be with me to help me process any painful news that might be coming. And, if there were any decisions to make, we would make them together because I had no idea what these ultrasounds and images would show. Since it was a Sunday, he had to skip church and decide what to tell the kids so they would not worry.

We waited all day for the results, and around 5:00 p.m., we got some answers. Jensyn's organs were normal looking and as healthy as they could be. They did not see what they anticipated they might see. Although the doctors were glad to know there was nothing wrong with her organs, the confusion about why she had low blood pressure, such a puffy body, and inconsistent fevers remained. Ultimately, they proposed that following the surgery, Jensyn had acquired aspiration pneumonia (wet lungs) and that her blood pressure issues might have been medicine-related. There was no answer to the swelling, just the hope that it would eventually go away. Overall, no definitive answer was far more acceptable than what we had expected to hear instead.

In response to this, I wrote on her CaringBridge:

November 28, 2022

Yesterday morning was hard. We had to wonder if having back-to-back-to-back-to-back UTIs was too much for her body. Did she even have enough strength to keep fighting? Before Chris came, Jensyn and I had a little heart-to-heart. We definitely do not want her to suffer, but we also want to say that we have done everything possible to keep her alive and with us.

I took her sweet, puffy-cheeked face into my hands and told her that we are not ready to let her go. Obviously, we will never be ready for that day. But, we want to see what this surgery can do for her. Her spine surgery was a risk, and it paid off nicely for her quality of life. This surgery, though not as risky, is going to do so much to reduce her infections. That, coupled with med changes, could make a huge difference in how she feels on the daily. We are here for it. I told her we want her to be here for it, too.

I know she listens to her mama—we have that kind of relationship. I also know that someday, when she has fought the good fight, we will know it. That has always been our prayer for her: that she will let us know, loud and clear. Jensyn is a fighter, and more than that, she has an army of many who fight for her with us! I say it all the time—I don't know how to even explain it, but we can FEEL the prayers where Jensyn is concerned. It is a supernatural peace that overwhelms and sustains. We are eternally grateful for it.

We were in the hospital until December 1, when we were discharged with another new diagnosis. Infectious disease doctors began to work closely with us. They discovered that Jensyn's overall health was being affected by *C. diff—Clostridioides difficile*—a germ or bacterium that causes diarrhea and colitis, which is inflammation of the colon. We were grateful that they were able to assess the situation and test for this clingy and frustrating new twist in her health journey. *C. diff* is super contagious and is not easy to fight. Either way, we felt like this was our answer to her issues, so we were willing to do whatever it would take to get rid of it. That, along with doing what we could to help her vesicostomy site heal, became a full-time endeavor, yet we were hopeful that things would eventually right themselves and 2023 would be a year of reprieve for our girl.

Some might say that she did get her reprieve in 2023, and even though we knew that Jensyn's life expectancy was always in question, what happened next rocked our world. And we did not see it coming.

BRUTALLY BEAUTIFUL

The first two months of 2023 were steady and full. Jensyn's immunologist prescribed weekly infusions for us to administer at home to build her immune system, we still walked hand-in-hand with urology as we combatted UTIs even with her vesicostomy, and Jensyn continued to live up to her "sleepy sloth" moniker. The underlying expectation was that she was still reeling from November and eventually would rebound from her surgery and subsequent *C. diff* diagnosis.

At the end of February, I had a milestone birthday and was thrilled to celebrate with my entire family—we played games, ate great food, and just hung out together all day. We also watched a video tribute Chris compiled for me with sentiments from a bunch of my friends and family. It was such a thoughtful gift. Since it was a big birthday and since I am one to declare my birthday should last the entire month, Chris extended the fun into the next day. What a gift it was to spend another entire day with my family. We went shopping, visited an escape room (we escaped with time to spare), and ended our time at my favorite pizza place. If only Jensyn could have been with us. That would have made the day perfect!

Chris's parents had agreed to stay at the house with Jensyn, and toward the end of the day, they called to tell us they needed to be on their way home. In my mind, this meant the birthday festivities were finished, and mentally I had moved on to what needed to be done for the week ahead. When my van of people (with our big crew, there are always multiple cars when we have an outing) was close to home, I remember being frustrated with the little girls who were bickering in the back seat. Maci and Sidney were also in my car and were trying to keep my mood light. But then, when we got home, I wanted to drive up to my mailbox to get my mail. Annoyingly, there were cars parked all over the street. "Ugh! I am so tired of the neighbors having these parties and parking their cars in front of my mailbox," I said. I had no idea the girls were recording my rant. It was not until I got into the house that I realized the party was for me! I had never had a surprise party before, and it was such a special time with people I adore! There was so much to be excited about, and I was hopeful that turning fifty really would be fantastic.

Exactly two weeks after my birthday, I was at the dentist, and Sidney was at the house working with Jensyn. Shortly after I finished at the dentist, I ran some errands. Sidney called to check in. While we were chatting, she went into Jensyn's room and saw that the back of Jensyn's head was dripping blood. Immediately, we Facetimed so I could see what she meant. I cut my errands short and hurried home. Upon closer examination, we realized there were other wounds of differing sizes on her head. We tried to clean the biggest one and realized that things were more severe than we originally thought. It was a bloody mess. Something was definitely wrong with Jensyn.

Jensyn's timing was not great once again. Chase and Maci's Gender Reveal Party was set to happen that night, and Chase's family had flown in to be part of it. Since it was just a few sores on her head and nothing more critical had presented itself, we opted to keep her home until after the night's festivities.

Blue and pink balloons. Raspberry and blueberry fritter French toast. Pink and blue cupcakes. Nine people were Team Blue. Seven sported the color of Team Pink. Before long, it was time to find out the good news. Maci had bought a fun, interactive game from Etsy that resulted in one winner who got to open a gift revealing the colored hat and pacifier that would spill the beans.

Team Blue earned bragging rights, and I was thrilled that another grandson was coming!

Shortly after the reveal, Chris and I decided to call for an ambulance transport. Not knowing what could be causing the sores on her head and believing that Jensyn continued to be sleepier than usual, we agreed it was time for her to get checked out. We headed back to St. Paul Children's. I was a mess when the ambulance showed up. Not only was I leaving during a celebration with my family and our new family from Tennessee, but the paramedic who tended to Jensyn questioned me in a way I had never been questioned before. He believed that someone had intentionally hurt Jensyn to cause the wounds on her head, and he directed his suspicion toward me. It was beyond peculiar that none of us had seen these sores before this time, but neglect and harm have never been words to define our care of Jensyn. She was watched and tended to around the clock.

Jensyn was routinely admitted to the fifth floor, and a flurry of tests were done, the labs drawn. The results were not definitive, but one of her enzymes was off-the-charts high, which led to a diagnosis of pancreatitis. Her pain was controlled, and nothing else seemed to be particularly concerning—except for the lesions on her head. Throughout Jensyn's journey, I was always amazed at the different types of professions in the world of doctors. Before Jensyn, I did not know there were doctors specializing in wounds. Wound care doctors are weirdly fascinated by lesions, which, in turn, fascinated me. Jensyn's new round of wounds was particularly interesting to our favorite wound care doctor, but she didn't know what was causing them. She did have a plan for treating them, so we were grateful for that.

The fifth floor is where patients are sent for noncritical issues. The first day, we were hanging out on Floor 5, and Jensyn was being monitored by her team. Around 5:23 a.m., Floor 5 could no longer handle Jensyn. Our nurse called Floor 4 (the dreaded PICU) to see if they had any "admittability." Jokingly, the nurse from fourth floor, who knew Jensyn was in the building, said, "Yes. But only if you are calling for Jensyn." She was kidding. Our nurse was not. Jensyn was transferred to the PICU.

Initially, I did not understand why they decided to transfer her. Jensyn was at the hospital for sores on her head and possibly pancreatitis, but the issue that had triggered her transfer was Jensyn's teeny, tiny veins. The lab techs were having trouble drawing enough blood, so the decision was made to put in a central line for easier access. I accepted that as a smart, efficient move—even at 5:30 in the morning.

Floor 4. So many memories on that floor. Emotions, thoughts, and tears—so many pieces of our lives had been left on that floor. Even more specific than Floor 4 was Room 2. In 2020, Room 2 housed our hearts for 40 days.

And Room 2 is where they welcomed us again. PTSD aside, I figured we would greet our medical family and do things differently this time.

As soon as we got situated, I called Chris to tell him things had been shaken up. Not believing things to be critical, he taught Sunday School, went to church, and then came to the hospital. At the time, things were stable, but as the day went on, Room 2 was hopping. Jensyn had high sodium, low blood pressure, yucky blood gasses, and several other concerning issues. Things had changed from somewhat stable to confusingly critical.

Dr. Kruse shared that things were not moving in the right direction. The main issue was that she was getting sicker and sicker, and there was no known reason for it. The labs and the tests and the scans were not adding up. There was a piece—the answer—missing. She said if things continued to trend as they were, we might have some not-so-easy decisions to make. Even though Jensyn's breathing was not an issue, the increased fluids and medications they gave were concerning enough that the lungs could be compromised at some point. Dr. Kruse believed there was a very real possibility that Jensyn would be intubated by the next morning.

After meeting with the doctor, I wrote this on Jensyn's CaringBridge:

March 5, 2023

*Floor 4! As much as we need you, we don't really like
you. You make us feel things we don't want to feel. You
create memories that hurt. Your couches are not comfy,
and your tissues are scratchy. For today, you are too
much for me. We miss you, Floor 5!*

*We know that God has chosen Floor 4 for our girl at
this time. We prayed for wisdom, and He gave it. We
prayed for comfort, and Jensyn has been more than
cared for. As much as we dislike so many parts of
Floor 4 and what it stands for, the people of Floor 4 are
God's gift to our girl. Attentive. Alert. Compassionate.
Caring. Family.*

*Jensyn was getting sick at home; once again, she is
SICK! God can redeem this sickness and save our girl.
He did it in Room 2 two years ago, and we believe He
will do it again.*

That was March 5. There was no intubation on
March 6 like the doctor predicted, but there were also
no answers as to what was causing Jensyn's health to
continue to decline. Over the years, people told me I could
consider myself a nurse based on everything I knew and

had done. Being a nurse is a big responsibility. Being a mom-nurse is a calling. I had learned many, many things about medical care, but what I knew was based on what was needed to know to keep Jensyn alive. I had become pretty good at reading and understanding blood work and test results—those EEGs and brain scans? Nope! Those take a special level of skill to master, and I had no hope of ever interpreting those. But bloodwork? Lab levels? I had a basic understanding of good numbers and those that were not. I knew certain numbers needed to go up and others needed to come down. By her sixth year of life, their technology finally started to color code these numbers, which helped me notice the different types of results more quickly. Everyone knows red is bad, and many of Jensyn's lab results were written in red. I woke up each morning, checking for a better level, a different color. The feeling of dread hovered. Yet, I still had hope. This was Jensyn, and Jensyn exceeds expectations; Jensyn always rebounds.

On March 7, we got more answers. Jensyn was sicker than we realized when they moved us to the PICU. Because Jensyn's body was getting septic again, they gave her a powerful med, Vancomycin, which presented a risk of injuring the kidneys. This injury happened in Jensyn, which meant her kidneys could not take in what her body needed. The condition is normally fixable, but the body has to wake up and do its part. Time is often what is needed for complete healing. The doctors also decided that Jensyn should be done with the ketogenic diet. This was a huge decision and was not an easy transition. Her condition and what happened next is best summed up in what would end up being my final journal entry to my girl.

March 9, 2023

> *You are officially six and a half years old today. And what a crazy six-and-a-half years it has been. You have been such a blessing, and you have never felt like a burden to our family. It has always been a privilege to care for you.*
>
> *You are so sick right now, Jensyn. You have been critically sick before, but your body has always had enough reserve to fight. We knew someday that would not be the case. And you are not getting better right now. Dad and I are so sad, and we know there will be more decisions to make in the future.*
>
> *That bladder of yours! It has failed you so many times and now has caused you to go into shock with sepsis once again. Because your body was in shock, they gave you a big drug, and the risk of that big drug is that it could harm your kidneys. Your sweet, weak kidneys*

got injured and are not bouncing back. You also have super low blood pressure, making your heart work harder. This is all catching up with your lungs, and you are struggling. We do not believe you are suffering, but we also know that more intervention, like a breathing tube, won't help you.

We have always said you would let us know when you were ready to go meet Jesus, but now that you might be telling us that, we don't want you to go, and we are not ready to hear it.

Jensyn! I am so much better at keeping you alive than letting you go. I know how to help you live—well, except for now when you are so sick—but I have absolutely no idea how to let you go. My heart is broken.

Your siblings are coming to see you today. This will be hard for them, but it has to be. We all need each other. Denice came last night and wants to come again today. The doctors and nurses here love you in such a special way. Your nurse from last night opted to stay to work some of today because even she has fallen in love with you in the three nights she has had you. You affect people, and you are such a gift.

Our family has done our best to be a witness during your journey, and that has been the best part—being able to show others God's glory because of you. We will continue to share your life, Jensyn—it has meant everything to us.

We know that God could still choose to heal you and that people—so many people— are praying for that to happen. But we can also understand why God would want you with Him—you are that amazing. For you to be with Jesus and to be able to run and dance and sing—I want that for you, too. Selfishly, we do not want to let you go, but we want whatever is best for you.

We will cherish this time with all the people who love you, and then we will follow your lead and the wisdom of Jesus to know our next steps. I have a lot more journal to fill, sweet girl—I am more than happy to keep writing!

We will do whatever it takes . . .
Love,
Mom

THERE WERE TEARS, BUT THERE WAS ALWAYS HOPE.

On March 9, Dr. Kruse approached us early in the day and told us that things were still not moving in the right direction for Jensyn. Her kidneys were failing. Her body was filling up with fluid, and her heart was having to work too hard. Her lungs were not keeping up as well as they had been before. We had decisions to make. Barring a miracle, Jensyn was dying. We agreed not to intubate and not to resuscitate. We Facetimed the kids and told them to come.

The kids came, along with Linda and Lowell. They each spent some time sitting at the bedside with their sister. Unfortunately, some of them had not understood the urgency of this visit. We shared that we would most likely be saying goodbye to Jensyn in the very near future. There were tears. But there was always hope—she had rallied so many times before. We spent time together, and then the kids went home, knowing they would likely return in the coming days.

Denice had been there to see Jensyn the night before. It was a special night because Jensyn had woken up a bit. Chris and I interacted with her in a way that we had been unable to for some time. She looked at us, listened to us, squeezed our hands, and responded. It was a gift, and at the time, it gave us a bit of hope. When Denice called to check on Jensyn the next day, we shared what the doctor had said and that we had made the painful decision to not offer life-saving options. She wanted to come back to see Jensyn again and to assess whether or not she needed to say her own goodbye. While she was there, Dr. Brockman, the new overnight intensivist and the same doctor who had been with us when we almost lost Jensyn in 2020, came to see us. He was surprised that Jensyn was still alive. He assumed she would have died before he came on shift. He believed that even if we did not take away her support, she would not make it through the night.

Devastated. Destroyed. Dumbfounded. I asked him why nobody else had told us this. I told him our children had already been there and left. I begged him to tell us we would have enough time for them to come back before we lost her. He did not have great answers, but he believed it was serious enough to have the kids return to the hospital. Denice, who heard all this, asked the other questions I could not formulate. Aside from being Jensyn's nurse, she was also a hospice nurse. After the doctor left, we asked for her opinion. She agreed with the doctor. Jensyn was not going to live much longer. She believed that the night before, when Jensyn was responsive and interactive with Chris and me, was her "rally night." Such a moment often happens before a person dies.

The kids had only been home for half an hour (we live a little over an hour from the hospital) when we called to tell them to come back. Max and Sidney were at their house, Tygen was at a girls' basketball game with his friends, Chase and Maci were at their apartment in Monticello, and the rest had returned to our house. Chase and Maci drove to Buffalo to get Tygen, and the rest loaded up to come back to us. We told them we would do whatever we could to sustain her until they arrived. We fervently prayed she would hold on. We sent word to our prayer warriors, asking them to uphold us, telling them we believed it was Jensyn's time. And we spent every minute we had left with our Jensy Marce.

Chris and I were frustrated the kids had already been there and left, and we could only hope they would make it back in time. There was nothing else they could do medically to keep her alive, so they brought in a bigger bed so we could crawl in and cuddle her. As difficult as it was to wonder if the kids would make it back, Chris and I saw the time we had, just the two of us, for the gift it was. We had to say goodbye to our daughter. As parents, we wanted to be strong for our family. Without the kids there, we had the chance to break down and cry and say all the things we needed to say as Jensyn's mom and dad. It was an ordained time. It was priceless.

Lowell and Linda and the kids made it back in time. Word spread to our church family. Two of our elders, Joe and Tucker, came to pray with us. Later, another elder, Jerry, and his wife, Karen, came to show their support.

Someone Facetimed my mom since she was not able to be there in person. She was recovering from hip surgery, but she and my dad still wanted to be part of Jensyn's final moments with all of us. The hospital room was full, the atmosphere heavy. The

"WE'RE DOING EVERYTHING WE CAN."

medical team continued to serve Jensyn despite what was coming. At one point, Britlyn approached Jensyn's respiratory therapist and said, "Can you save my sister?"

"We're doing everything we can," he said. Britlyn was beginning to see the severity of what was happening.

As I took in the room, life felt surreal. I have never had an out-of-body experience, but this felt like one. As I witnessed each of my children sobbing as they cuddled in bed with their baby sister, it felt like a nightmare. At the same time, it felt like one of the proudest moments of my life. The dichotomy of pain and pride left a pit in my gut and a swelling in my heart that was indescribable.

Dr. Brockman was waiting for our cue to take the next step. We could have chosen to let her pass on her own during the night, but there is no closure in that. We wanted to be with her until her last breath. There was no other way to do that but to take away her support and hold her until the end. Yet, we felt no urgency. So, the weird awkwardness in the room continued. At one point,

Joe felt the need to do something. "Is anyone hungry?" he asked.

Collectively, the kids admitted they had not eaten supper. Knowing the cravings of a pregnant woman, Joe asked Maci if there was something she was hungry for. "Canes," she said.

Joe left to get chicken, and we continued to cuddle, reminisce, and talk about everything and nothing at the same time. It was getting late—almost 9:00 p.m. at this point. However, there was no way we were going to sit around Jensyn's bed and munch on chicken and fries while watching her last moments. Once Joe returned, and when all those who could stomach food had eaten, Chris and I decided it was time.

We called in Dr. Brockman and Jensyn's nurse, Sara. Then, we crawled into the bed, and our kids surrounded us and their sister. They put Jensyn in my arms—the first time since she was two months old that she was untethered. No more oxygen. No more feeding tube. No more support. The only thing she still had was an IV because they needed to administer a med to keep her comfortable as her body shut down. Since they had to give Dilaudid (a pain medication) in intervals as Jensyn presented her need, it often felt too intentional when they would push the button, and it proved to be confusing to Britlyn. At one point, she looked at Chris and screamed, "Why are you letting them kill your daughter?" We could see her little heart breaking as she attempted to reconcile what was happening with her sister. In hindsight, we maybe should have left the cannula in her nose—something that might have helped her look like Jensyn because her swollen body was somewhat unsettling to all of us.

We had absolutely no clue what to do at this moment. What do you do when you are holding your dying daughter? How do you wrap your head around what this all means? You have no words. There is nothing more to say. So we sang. We praised. We worshiped the One who was taking back our girl. Song after song after song. We had no playlist. There was no plan. But God. Each song was perfect. Each lyric was a testimony to what Jensyn's life had been. Each voice, each upraised hand, each heart of worship was sacrificed on that hospital bed. Jensyn was with us for another forty minutes before we sang the lyrics from Chris Tomlin's song "I Will Rise": *And I will rise when He calls my name; No more sorrow, no more pain."* She took her last breath at that very moment, at 12:36 a.m. on March 10, 2023.

It was brutal. It was beautiful. As a family, we had the privilege of taking our girl all the way to the gates of

> SO WE SANG. WE PRAISED. WE WORSHIPED THE ONE WHO WAS TAKING BACK OUR GIRL.

heaven; we had a taste of what heaven would someday be.
And Jesus met us there.

CELEBRATING LIFE

The days following Jensyn's death were beyond difficult. She really had been our everything. Our days revolved around caring for her, so in her absence, we did not know how to live. But we knew the only way to get through it was to go through it. And that is what we did. Together.

March 9 is a day we will never forget. March 10 was a day of loving, leaving, and loss. Both days, we saw God at work. But this loss hurt. Badly.

Life sure is funny sometimes. I remembered again what Dr. Brockman said in 2020 after we almost lost Jensyn the first time: "There will come a day when you will leave this hospital without Jensyn." The irony is that God chose Dr. Brockman to be our doctor at the end. Horrifically, and as irony would have it, I hated that his words came true. After Jensyn passed, we held her and grieved together for another hour. We sent the kids home, and Chris and I figured we would stick around to complete whatever needed to be done next. Chris left the room to speak with the doctor to determine what that would be. The doctor told us that we were to lay Jensyn on the bed, and we were free to go. They would take things from there.

Watching Jensyn die was beyond brutal. Laying her on a hospital bed and walking away from her, not knowing when I would see her again, was actually worse than excruciating. There is absolutely no word to describe it. One-eighth of my heart broke off completely, and at that point, I had no idea how it would ever possibly be whole again. To this day, leaving her and not tending to her one last time is my biggest regret. Oh, how I wish I had helped her nurse, Sara, clean her up and comb her hair and get her ready. I should have mothered her one more time. But I did not know that I could.

The one-hour trip home in a weird March snowstorm felt like five hours. There was no sleep that first night. All the girls were in our room because we truly needed to be together. We woke up in a nightmare that we could not shake, only to realize we needed to choose a funeral home and a church and begin to plan her service. By 1:00 in the afternoon on March 10, we had met with people to set the plans in motion. All I could think about was Jensyn, lying somewhere in a cold hospital, all by herself. I asked the woman at the funeral home at what point they would pick her up and bring her there. She replied that her partner was already en route and that Jensyn would be in their care within the hour. I felt better but hated that we were planning any of this.

The week after was busy and full and hard. We must have been in shock because autopilot kicked in, and we did what we had to do. There was no time to feel or to mourn or to really grieve at all. We switched gears to do what we could as a family to honor and celebrate our girl in the best way possible. I wrote her obituary—trying to encapsulate all that she was to us in her short six years of life was overwhelming. She did not have the accolades and accomplishments that a typical person has at the end of their life, but there was still so much we wanted to say as a tribute to her. We had to figure out other details— flowers from the family to go on the casket, where we wanted her to be buried in the cemetery, purchasing a casket, and so much more. As a family, we spent as much time with each other as possible and planned all the details

> WE SERVED JENSYN AS A TEAM, AND WE WOULD CELEBRATE HER AS A TEAM AS WELL.

together. It was weirdly therapeutic and comforting. We served Jensyn as a team, and we would celebrate her as a team as well.

Choosing what my child would wear and how she would look was very difficult for me. I had bought her a new dress for Easter—dark gray with pink and white flowers. I rarely bought Jensyn anything for special occasions, and I hardly ever bought her a dress. It was just not practical attire for her to wear in a wheelchair, but I loved this dress and was hopeful we would be able to go to the Easter service as a family, so I wanted her to look her best. Never did I think she would wear the dress for her funeral instead. Her hair was unruly and messy at the time of her passing. Few knew how to scrunch her curls properly to make her look like her adorable self, and as her mother, I wanted her to look like Jensyn as much as possible. Maci, Sidney, and I gave detailed instructions to those at the funeral home in an attempt to show them how to do it. On her big day, she looked absolutely beautiful, and I will always remember the relief I felt when I first saw her that day lying in her nondescript wooden casket, made lovingly for her by some monks in Iowa.

We did not know what to expect from her service, so we planned what we could. Our church family and friends were more than willing to help in any way. Anytime something came up, we asked for help, and the need was met. Our church did not have a senior pastor at that time, so we were uncertain about what to do for that part of her funeral service. After praying, we decided to ask Jerry Gudim, one of our current elders who has known our family for twenty years, and Joe Ley, another one of our elders who just happened to be there with us when Jensyn took her last breath. After Joe went to get Cane's the night of Jensyn's passing, he got "stuck" in the back of the hospital room. Chris and I had already set things in motion to pull Jensyn's support, and Joe felt it would be awkward for him to leave. As we started singing our first praise song, Lowell reached for Joe and pulled him over by him and Linda at the foot of the bed. Joe became part of our family that night, so who better to share about Jensyn's last moments than him?

Another special moment for me was to have my mentor, Marcia, share the closing prayer. Marcia was part of Jensyn's journey from the beginning, and it was more than fitting to have her there at the end. It was also a blessing to have Chase, her new brother-in-law, read her life verses from Psalm 139:13-18—to remind us all that it was God who had knit her together, that she was fearfully and wonderfully made, and that all her days were ordained for her before they came to be.

Our kids wanted to be part of the service. All seven of them, along with Sidney, felt they could honor Jensyn best by leading worship, which they regularly do for church. I could only imagine how difficult it was for them to sing worship songs in the atmosphere of their sister's funeral, but I was so grateful they wanted to do that for her. As we were deciding which songs to sing, we knew there were a few we had to include—"Gratitude" by Brandon Lake, "Goodness of God" by Jenn Johnson, and "I Will Rise" by Chris Tomlin. At one point, someone had the idea to look at the playlist history of the songs we had sung at the hospital. Tate had been our unofficial DJ that night and had chosen songs at random—each one so perfect for what we were going through at the time. Oddly enough, when we tried to find the recently played list, no record was found. We were left to believe it was another divine, ordained moment—one that would forever be special only to that night.

Since so many people had never officially met Jensyn, we also prepared a slideshow of photos. As we pulled together pictures, it became a sweet time of remembering and cherishing what our journey with Jensyn meant to us. Tate compiled the pictures, and we played the song Brinkley wrote for her sister called "Little Fighter." Brinkley wrote the song well before Jensyn's passing, and the final lyrics of the original song were:

She's a fighter, a survivor
A brave one, you see.
It's okay, It's all right

She will fight this fight
And she'll win this war, all right

After Jensyn passed, Brinkley re-recorded the song with different ending lyrics:

It's okay, It's all right
She fought her fight
And won her war, all right.

Such a sweet song and tribute to her sister. Maci also had written a song for Jensyn. At the end of the service, we played a video of her performing her piece entitled "Provision"—a song about trusting God to provide in the good times and hard times that our family had experienced over and over again.

Sunday, March 19, 2023, was Jensyn's Celebration of Life service. Our church meets at Becker High School, so we do not have our own building. Not sure how big of a crowd to expect, we were advised to have the funeral at Riverside Church in Big Lake, Minnesota. Over 550 people poured into the church that afternoon. We were overwhelmed and overjoyed. Seeing that much support for our girl, whom most had never physically met, was a true testimony of God's glory displayed in her life. There really was something special about Jensyn. She connected people. She challenged people. She showed people God is true and faithful and worthy of praise in all situations. We witnessed this every day of her six years and did our best to share that miracle with anyone who followed her journey.

We celebrated her LIFE: Live Intentionally For Eternity. The Lord had given Chris this acronym many years ago before a youth retreat, and the meaning behind it has been important to our family ever since. Jensyn's life was short. Jensyn's life was not easy. But Jensyn's life still matters for eternity, and that is what gave her worth and value for every minute that she lived.

Jensyn's interment was the following day in Becker. Our interim pastor, Jerry Deppa, led a small congregation of family and friends in a sweet time of prayer and praise. We played the song God gave Maci when Jensyn was born, and as we sang it together, we expressed our conviction that God truly is not finished with Jensyn yet. Yes, she is with Jesus, but her story is not complete just because she is no longer physically with us. Her memory, her mission, her massive impact will continue to live out in how we view our future and

HER MEMORY, HER MISSION, HER MASSIVE IMPACT WILL CONTINUE TO LIVE OUT IN HOW WE VIEW OUR FUTURE AND OUR ETERNITY.

our eternity. Yet, even with that knowledge, burying a child feels so final.

Like all the other hard things we anticipated when we first learned of Jensyn's diagnosis and prognosis, I so dreaded this day. Choosing a cemetery plot, paying a bunch of money to thaw the frozen ground so the caretaker could get it ready, and watching as they lowered her casket into a cold, cement vault felt like the ultimate culmination of life as we knew it, yet at the same time it was the birth of gut-wrenching, crippling grief.

When the sweet gal from the funeral home gestured to our family to gather around the casket to say our goodbyes, I recall feeling awkward and empty. As everyone else watched, we grabbed flowers from the casket cascade and presented them to Jensyn. We laid them on the wooden box that held the body of our girl. It felt too weird to say goodbye, to speak any words audibly. I knew Jensyn was not there. She would not hear our words. Saying something, anything, would not change our situation. So we remained quiet. We cried. We hugged. We finished what we set out to do. And, just like everything we have ever done, we did it together.

RIPPLE EFFECT

You might have a medically fragile child if—

1. Friends see an ambulance go by, and they text you to see if all is okay at your house.
2. Your eight-year-old knows the difference between a cannula and a catheter.
3. When shopping, you buy clothes based on whether they would be comfy enough for hanging out at the hospital.
4. Your children's play doctor kit contains authentic feeding bags, cannulas, syringes in many sizes, and an IV pole.
5. Your daughters ask for a feeding tube button to be put into one of their dolls so that it can be just like Jensyn.

6. *When you leave the hospital, you tell the nurses and staff that you will see them next time.*
7. *You have no idea what tomorrow holds, but you are so grateful for each day you already had.*

When our pastor asked us to share our story with our church family on Mother's Day in 2021, this is how Chris and I started our talk. Although somewhat comical, each of these things was a reality in our lives and in our home. We were fairly well versed in what it meant to have a medically fragile child, and although not everyone could relate on exactly the same level, people were able to see God at work.

After receiving Jensyn's diagnosis and once we got over the initial shock, we decided that our journey with her could only bring glory to God if we lived it openly and shared it with others. We have seen people's perspectives on the value of life or, in some cases, its lack of value. We have learned that life is not about healthy children but about how we react when given unhealthy children. We have learned that life is hard—not just for us but for everyone. We all have "hard" in our lives, and sometimes, when I have seen what others have for their hard, I would weirdly still choose mine. Every hospital stay, every ambulance ride, every missed opportunity, every frustrating day, every ignorant comment from doctors who thought we were selfish to keep Jensyn around—in

every. little. thing. we have maintained hope, and our goal
has been to show others our hope in Jesus. If God had
chosen to heal Jensyn, we would have taken that victory!
But even when healing was not the answer for our girl, we
chose to trust Him.

We have repeatedly witnessed God use Jensyn, and
over the years, He has allowed us to hear from people
about how she impacted them. When Jensyn was fighting
for her life in 2020, she had many nurses helping her in
that battle. So many sweet nurses became our friends
over the years. Tammy was a seasoned nurse and near
retirement. She had been a PICU nurse for over twenty
years, and there was a time many years ago when she
and her husband did respite care for kids like Jensyn so
that families could go on a trip or have a weekend break,
knowing their child was being cared for.

One day, after being Jensyn's nurse, Tammy told me
that she went home, told her husband about Jensyn, and
said that she felt they should get recertified to do respite
care again. Her husband agreed and was in the process of
finalizing things to care for medically special kids again.
She told me that because of HIPAA, she could not use
Jensyn's real name when she spoke about her to others,
so she referred to Jensyn as Baby Joy! It meant everything
to me that she took the time to share this and that God
would allow Jensyn to be used to affect lives in this way.

People of all ages loved our Jensy. We often heard from friends that their children would pray for Jensyn regularly, which always meant so much to us. Sidney's sister, Avery, shared about Jensyn in a paper she wrote for one of the classes I teach at our homeschool co-op.

Most people know who Jensyn is. Her life has brought amazing things to me and so many others. Everyone knows her and how she's made an impact. I never had a close connection to her, but in a way, I loved her.

I remember times when my family hosted the Salvevolds for the Super Bowl. I remember braiding Jensyn's hair and seeing her smiles. Even though I didn't know her very well, I know this: when Jensyn passed away, I realized for anyone who grieves her passing, everything has a plan and purpose. Even when we don't see God working, He is. And Jensyn's amazing life has brought me to see that even when we are lost in confusion and sadness, we can trust there is a purpose for everything.

Another student in our co-op, Aviana, actually felt led to write a song about Jensyn. She wrote the song, "Miracles," which talks about how Jensyn was

Six years of miracles
She was a miracle from the start
Never not a miracle
She's a warrior, a warrior
She never stopped fighting; never stopped being a
warrior.

This sweet ten-year-old's song went on to say that even when the doctors thought she was done, God saved her; He gave her more earthly time. He does miracles. Aviana not only wrote the lyrics but also wrote the music, which she recorded and shared with our family after Jensyn's passing. Aviana only met Jensyn once, but her family prayed for us daily.

Jensyn also confirmed the direction in Hannah's life. Hannah, one of our youth group girls, came with her mom to visit us in the hospital when Jensyn was a baby. She was just beginning college to become a nurse, so she was excited to be in that environment. She wrote this to us after Jensyn passed away:

I am thinking and praying for you all. I am so
encouraged by your hope in Christ all throughout
Jensyn's life. I am challenged by your example to
value life. Your family is such a beautiful example
of reflecting Christ as you value friends and family

in His image. I remember the first time I visited Jens in the hospital. It was so impactful for me. Talking with you about your experiences with nurses was so helpful. After leaving the hospital, I felt confident and excited about my decision to be a nurse. Thank you for glorifying God throughout Jensyn's life. I have thought about Jens as I have gone through nursing school. I hope to value life and care well for each patient I have, as you have all done. Thank you for including us in her journey.

It goes without saying that Jensyn had plenty of opportunities to impact the nurses at the Children's Hospitals. What a blessing it was to receive two handwritten sympathy cards signed by twenty-five nurses who cared for her. A simple word of condolence would have been meaningful enough, but their heartfelt memories of Jensyn meant so much.

Sending you love and prayers for your family for such a special girl. It was an honor to be part of Jensyn's final journey.—Sara, RN, who was with us when Jensyn passed away.

I am so honored to have cared for Jensyn over the years. I will always remember her cute voices and noises letting us know her thoughts. She is so special, and I will remember her always.—Lauren, RN

Jensyn was such a beautiful girl. I loved hearing her on the unit—you always knew when Jensyn was here. A joyous soul.—Kayla, RN

It was an honor to care for Jensyn. She was a sweetheart and loved by so many. I will always remember her and your beautiful family.—Corinne, RN

I always enjoyed taking care of your sweet Jensyn. Her voice is the sweetest.—Sara, RN

Jensyn was such a special girl. All the love was felt from your family to our staff whenever she was here. We will all miss her dearly.—Bianca, CSA

Thinking of Jensyn and your family. She was a special girl and will be missed. Thoughts and prayers with you all.—Brandon, RN

Jensyn was always a pleasure to care for. You could always feel the love in her room.—Nadine, RN

Another PICU nurse, Janessa, realized a few years ago that she and I are related. Because of this, she was not able to be Jensyn's nurse. However, as one of the charge nurses, she could assist the other nurses from time to time when we were in the hospital. After Jensyn passed, the Lord gave me the gift of her words as she shared her thoughts with me.

> *I'm so sorry for your loss. Know that we ALL LOVED JENSYN. The St. Paul PICU is a big family, and I made it clear that Jensyn was in some way both work family and biological family. In a weird and silent way, she helped me with my testimony and all the nurses on our unit knew this. We think of her often.*

> *We see each child in our care as one of our own children. The nurse who cared for Jensyn the night she passed was deeply affected. She is an amazing nurse and a woman I look up to. I heard it was absolutely beautiful. And her doctor is one of the most compassionate doctors we have. He genuinely cares and loves each patient as his own.*

> *We are a family for sure, and we love every family our care touches. One night or many months, we treat our patients as our own. Thank you for blessing us with time with Jensyn.*

As much as those at the hospital miss our girl, we miss them as well. After spending so much time with them for so many days at a time, relationships develop. This was just another area where we grieved loss.

Aside from those in the medical world, we would often get a text from someone we had not seen in a while or a message on Facebook or her CaringBridge saying that Jensyn had impacted a life in some way. These people had often never met Jensyn, yet they told us they felt like they knew her. People from all over followed our story, and we were the recipients of God's hand at work through their prayers, care, concern, and encouragement as we walked our journey. As much as God used Jensyn's story to impact other lives, He allowed people to greatly affect our lives at the same time. She was the great connection between people and us—some we never would have met without her and others who came back into our lives because of her. All of it became a blessing and is part of God's story with our girl.

Amid all of the hard days, there has been undeniable proof of God's fingerprints on many areas. Although we are grateful for the connections made with people outside our family, watching what Jensyn did in our family was the best example of God's love and mercy. I have never been more proud of my kids than seeing how they responded to their sister. They adored her, and when her pulmonologist told me that I was suffering, that my kids were suffering, that this fight was too much for us, I meant it when I told her that giving up on Jensyn would be the worst kind of suffering for my kids.

Jakely loved just spending time with her sister. After Jensyn passed away, she wrote this:

Jensy Marce—I miss you so much. I know you're in a better place now, but I miss reading to you, I miss seeing you smile, and I miss giving you baths and holding you. I even miss changing your diapers. I miss going outside with you and Sidney when we would lie on the grass and play games. I miss coming home and running to your room to see you. I miss everything about you.

Love,
Jakely

Brinkley also cherished any time she could get with Jensyn.

Life has been crazy without you, Jensyn. It feels like yesterday you passed, but it also feels like decades ago. You were such a light, and I love and miss you. I am still writing music, and two of my songs are for you. I am so excited to write more.

I miss you so much. You'll always be in my heart, Jensy Marce. You made me a better person. I wish I could hold you one more time. I miss hearing you chat. I miss fighting over who gets to hold you. I miss everything and would take it back any day. You were amazing at being a sister, and I will always love you.

Love,
Brinkley

Never had the kids seen Jensyn as a burden. They never complained that we could not do things as a family because of Jensyn. Never had they wanted anything but for us to fight for their sister. "Never" might seem too strong of a word, maybe even an unrealistic word to say in this situation, and some might wonder if there ever was a time when "never" was actually not true. If there was, it was not mentioned, articulated, or known. Instead, each of them cherished any time they could get with their sister. They sacrificed time with me and Chris. They gave up having friends over and knew we could not take family trips. They prayed for her and served her and fought over who got to spend time with her. It was unlike any sibling relationship I have ever seen, and in the process, their relationships with each other got stronger as well.

Over the years, I do believe I saw the kids suffer from time to time, but only as they watched their sister struggle. When I remember them sitting beside her hospital bed after being awakened in the wee hours of the morning, unsure of what they were walking into, my heart was heavy, yet full. In their pain and uncertainty, they embraced the time they had with Jensyn, understanding that only God knew the number of her days. They took turns sitting beside her, praying for her, crying with her, and just being with her. As a mom, seeing them struggle in the midst of her struggle sometimes felt unfair. But again, their great love for her was an example to me and is a picture of something beautiful I will forever hold close to my heart.

Maci wrote this about her sister a few days after she passed away, and she shared it at Jensyn's funeral.

March 13, 2023

Jensyn was my hardest lesson but my greatest blessing. Throughout her life, the Holy Spirit taught me so much about who God is through her. I quickly learned that I could not rely on my own strength. As much hardship was brought around, joy was abundantly more present with her. The way she interacted with everyone was unique, but her joy did not change.

I was holding Jensyn when she laughed for the first time; I was also holding her when she had her first seizure. Jensyn and I always had a special connection. I don't know if I can really explain it, but somehow we understood each other.

She always knew me and could always tell when I walked into her room or if I was holding her. I always thought of her as my healing buddy. If I was having a bad day, I'd cuddle up next to her, and somehow, we'd both calm down.

I will never forget the impact Jensyn has had on me. I'll never forget how she could light up a room. She taught me how to love somebody without getting love back. She loved us in her own way, but not the way the world has known. She perfectly displayed the Gospel somehow.

Sidney's connection as her sister-in-law and caretaker was so unique. She wrote this in her letter to Jensyn at our celebration of her first heavenly birthday:

September 9, 2023

I often think about you and about how different life is without you with us. I miss you so much. I miss you talking to me every day when I'd come over to take care of you. I wish you were able to be with my kids. Crosby remembers you, but Sadie never will, and it makes me sad.

I still feel like I don't know what to do without you here to take care of. You gave me such a purpose in life. I loved to take care of you. I know you are in a better place now, but we are all a little jealous and wish you were here with us. I love you, Jensy Marce. If you were here, I'd give you the longest birthday bath!

And, although Chase was not part of Jensyn's life for as long as everyone else, Jensyn made an impact on him as well.

Hey Jensy -

It's been a few months since you got to go hang out with Jesus forever. I'm super jealous that you get to be in His presence. Though, we also wish you were here with us. It's been hard without you here.

I wish I could ask you what you did to comfort Maci. You were always the best at it. I am trying to take over the reins, but it gets hard. I don't know what to do other than hold her tight.

*Thanks for letting me marry her and for your approval.
I start nursing school soon. I was looking forward to
helping take care of you. Can't wait to meet again,
Jensy Marce.*

*Love your favorite brother-in-law,
Chase*

Even in their grief, the kids have been able to embrace these days as an opportunity for reflection and praise as well—another testimony of God's work through Jensyn in their lives. Max's words to his sister serve as an excellent example of this.

Dear Jensyn,

It feels like it's been forever, and it also feels like I just held you yesterday. In that way, I don't know if a lot has happened since you passed or if nothing really has. Mace, Mom, and Sid often send pictures of you to our family chat, and it always feels like a mixture of joy and agony.

Since we gave you to Jesus, I have continued to fall in love with worship leading. I think the most true I've ever been with my worship is the last time I was with you—when we all just praised from the depths of our souls. None of our emotions or fleshly desires seemed to align with the words we sang, but I have never meant the words more. I'm sure I will spend every day trying to replicate that night. I think I'll be with you again the next time I worship like that. I love you, Jensyn. I can't wait to hear your voice sing with ours on that day.

Love,
Max

In the aftermath of losing their sister, Tate and Tygen also exposed their hearts for Jensyn.

Hey Jensy -

How's heaven? I have zero doubt in my mind that it's amazing. We can't wait to see you finally walk. What happened when you first saw Jesus? I bet He was so proud to see you.

Jensyn, you have been such a huge part of our family, and I'm so happy that I was able to be your brother. You made our family so close, and I can't wait for us all to be reunited.

Love,
Tate

Alright, Jensy. Life has been way different since March 10. There's not a day I don't miss you. We aren't doing great living without you. Miss you so much, girly, and I can't wait to meet you in heaven. Love you so much!

Love,
Big Bro Tygen

Even Britlyn, the sister of few words, expressed her love and loyalty for Jensyn the best way she knows how in the wake of her passing when she wrote:

Hi Jensyn. I miss you, and I love you.

Love you,
Britlyn

Yes, Jensyn's unintentional ripple effect miraculously reached far and wide, a fact for which we are grateful. But for her life and story to not greatly affect our own family would have felt like such a missed blessing. As Maci said, Jensyn taught us how to love without getting tangible love back. Instead, she left us with a deeper understanding of what it means to cherish each other, to embrace hard things, and ultimately to grieve with gratitude because life is about so much more than existing. It is about pressing into that unconditional love and mercy only a perfect God can give—about sharing the Gospel in everything we do, even when, sometimes, we have no words.

LOSS IS LOUD

For six and a half years, our days were dictated by serving Jensyn. To be honest, there were times I wondered what life would be like after she passed. Would I feel a sense of freedom? Would I appreciate more time to do things without restriction to my schedule? Would I feel relief from the constant worry and uncertainty? Yet, each time one of those thoughts crossed my mind, the genuine nausea in the pit of my stomach was enough to drive them away. I loved caring for Jensyn, but in my humanity, I had considered what life would be like without her—not because I wanted it that way but because I knew someday she would be gone.

It has been nothing like how I wondered it might be. My schedule has freedom, but I hate every minute of it. I am glad not to worry about her health or whether she is struggling, but I miss the many hours of focusing on her.

I feel zero relief. I do not know what to do with my days, and losing her is just the tip of the insane amount of loss we have endured. Grief is no joke. The person who passes definitely gets the better end of the proverbial bargain because the rest of us are left behind to figure out how to live again, yet even then it feels like our own kind of death.

Some of my journal entries from the week after her funeral best show how I felt at the time.

Tuesday, March 21, 2023

We all feel lost and off today. This feeling is difficult to explain. Everything now feels "over," and we don't know what to do or how to feel. The kids feel the same way. I have all this time on my hands, and I was really good at caring for Jensyn. I am not sure what my role in life is right now. Things are just weird all over.

Thursday, March 23, 2023

The days do not get easier. Emotionally and physically, I am just weary. This is so hard. I should be able to be productive, but instead, I am brain fatigued and cannot get motivated to do much of anything. I began to clean out Jensyn's room today. I do NOT want to do this.

Friday, March 24, 2023

Still so emotional! I do not feel like myself, which annoys me. Someone suggested that maybe I have lost my purpose—that is so accurate. Sidney and Maci are floundering as well. We keep pressing on.

Losing Jensyn has been the most difficult thing I have ever had to endure in my life. And though nothing else compares to it, there was more loss to grieve. Sidney and the grandkids stopped coming to our house to work. Suddenly, she was without a job and became a mom who now stays at home with her kids. I miss Sidney, and we feel her absence and that of the kids in our home. Maci also lost her job with Jensyn. Most of the time, when someone dies, employment is not connected to that person. When Jensyn passed, the three of us lost the income we received for taking care of her, and that unexpected reality has been life-changing, so much so that Maci and Chase actually moved in with Max and Sidney. This was financially beneficial for all of them, and of course, we love that all of our kids live so close to us (their house is just three blocks from ours) and that they love each other enough to live together. Obviously, Denice lost her "boss" as well. And, because Denice's connection to Jensyn was so strong, she chose not to continue nursing. After working with a couple of other kids for a few months, Denice

LOSS.
GRIEF.
THEY FEEL
THE SAME.

decided that losing Jensyn was enough to wreck her for nursing. She is now working for Make-A-Wish, using what she learned from Jensyn to bless other boys and girls. Although Denice will always be part of our family, we miss her—more loss.

Loss. Grief. They feel the same. Loss is painful, and I have a very high pain tolerance. Yet, adding grief to pain makes it hard to breathe, impossible to fully function. Shortly after Jensyn passed, Denice asked me how I was feeling. I told her that my heart physically hurt, that my soul felt empty. She told me a broken heart is a real thing. Unlike a broken bone, however, a heart cannot be patched. It just stays shattered.

I have learned that everyone processes grief differently, and however we process it is right and okay. At one point, I commented that I wanted to figure out stuff and move on. I was challenged to think about that concept differently, however, which meant everything for my mindset. The words "moving on" imply that I have left Jensyn behind and am trying to figure out life without her. Instead, I should do what I can to "move forward." Moving forward recognizes that Jensyn is still a part of me as I seek to unravel this reality. Yes. Moving forward, someday out of the grip of grief, makes at least some movement possible. With that renewed vision, I began the process of going through and getting rid of Jensyn's things.

"Mom, why did you empty Jensyn's cupboard?" Tygen asked me this question shortly after Jensyn passed away. One kitchen cupboard and a drawer were designated as Jensyn's and were filled with her special formula, her many bottles of medication, and other excess supplies. While the boys were gone at a hockey game the weekend after her passing, I could not even bear to be in that room—the reminders of Jensyn were too much for me. So, I grabbed a bag and pulled everything out. I filled the spaces with other things and thought nothing more of it. When I saw my son in tears, I knew that how we handled grief and what we decided to do with Jensyn's things would be another area where we needed to work together. While it unsettled me to see those reminders in the kitchen, their sudden absence upset Tygen.

Believing Jensyn's equipment and supplies could benefit another and, in return, honor her, we did what we could to donate and sell the things we no longer needed. My friend, Nicole, reached out to offer help with this overwhelming endeavor. We had absolutely no idea where even to begin, and we were so grateful for her help. Her room was a constant reminder that she was gone. For a while, we kept things intact. Yet, we knew she was not coming back, and it became difficult for me to see her room empty every day. The girls and I had spent so much time creating the perfect space for her when she was alive, but once her medical bed was gone, it felt emptier than ever. It was time for her room to become my office again. It is still my favorite room in our house—we spent so much time with her in this space. And, as I have written her story and reflected on her life through journals, files, and documents, it still feels like she and I are doing this together. Her memory lives on in this place—bistro lights on the ceiling, mementos of her scattered on the shelves, photos of our family together, and her super large sloth, Briggs, suspended in his hammock in the corner of the room—I still feel her here.

As a mother, dealing with my own grief has often felt like too much, yet worrying about how my children are handling their heartbreak became all-consuming. I have heard that grieving is like having broken ribs: we look fine on the outside, but with every breath, it hurts. And it hurts badly. So, if I am feeling that way, how are my kids feeling? And is it okay for them to see me looking fine on the outside without knowing how crippled I am on the inside? Our home had a rhythm when Jensyn was alive. It did not fall into a consistent cadence right away, but we figured out each person's choreography over time, and everyone knew their steps. The dissonance that came with grief, however, took us out of formation, and neither

Chris nor I knew how to fix it. I explained it this way on her CaringBridge.

April 5, 2023

Losing Jensyn is a different kind of broken and an uglier, emptier kind of grief than her initial diagnosis. But it still feels like a dance. The problem is that everyone is doing different steps this time—none of us seems to hear the same beat. Sometimes, the music is too loud, and my mind cannot concentrate; sometimes, the music is missing, and there is no count to follow. All of the time, I feel out of sync with what is happening around me as I want so badly to be present with the others in my life, but I cannot even decipher what my next move should be. The dissonance is deafening, and I yearn for our family to figure out this new choreography, to be in rhythm once again.

Time. I know it takes time. And dancing is all about timing. Obviously, we have never done this dance before, and we are learning as we go. It is true when they say everyone processes death differently. And maybe that is what will someday make this dance something beautiful. Maybe the goal is not to do the same dance but to trust that God has a different dance for each of us. He will teach us the steps it takes for

*us to regain our rhythm and to hear the music once
again. And when we all get to that point, our dancing
won't have to be in perfect sync because it will be an
expression of our journey and a witness to the One
who was our partner through it all. And we will still do
it together—one step at a time.*

Together. That has always been a focus for our family,
and because of that, Chris and I knew grieving Jensyn was
another area where we would need each other. It became
obvious to us that it was not okay for the broken parts
to remain hidden because sheltering the kids from the
shattered pieces leaves sharp, rough edges that only cause
more pain. We have been told that the only way to heal it
is to feel it. But feeling it hurts.

THREATENED ONENESS

Parenting a medically fragile, special-needs child is all-consuming in the best of circumstances. We have lived in survival mode for much of the past ten years as we cared for our two unique daughters—all while trying to make life for our other kids as normal as possible. The funny thing about survival mode is that we did what we needed to do to meet the needs of everyone else, but when things started to unravel, we were able to see what was left—what was barely holding together at times. Once again, what was presented on the outside was not what was happening on the inside—we just did not know it at the time.

I never want to project that we are a perfect family or that our marriage is without conflict. Truly, a family cannot endure what we have gone through and come out of it unscathed. When Chris and I got married, we chose a motto for our union: "Our Oneness Will Be Our

Witness." That has always been our goal, the benchmark of our marriage, and the heart of our family. We worked hard during our first years to lay a foundation of belief in each other and of faith in God. This has carried us through many hard times, and I believe that because of this foundation, we have been able to endure the challenging years of caring for Jensyn and, ultimately, find support from it in her death.

Even though our days were marked by making Jensyn comfortable and cared for, Chris continued to do ministry at church. He often felt pulled in several directions while doing his best to disciple the students and fulfill the expectations of his job. No church is perfect, and ours went through a difficult period over the course of a few years, which only added to Chris's stress. Things were taking a toll, and then we lost Jensyn.

Before Jensyn passed away, Chris read a book about preventing burnout in pastors. Knowing we needed to decompress and discuss what we had gone through, he reached out to the place mentioned in the book—a place designed for pastors and their wives who need to refresh, refuel, and reflect through a time of counseling and group therapy. This program was very expensive, and Chris knew we could not swing it financially. Not only was the retreat costly, but we would also need money for airfare and other expenses. Initially, he told them we could not attend. A week later, the man who wrote the book personally emailed Chris. After reading about our situation, he told Chris about a woman on their board who had just lost her granddaughter. She said if a pastor who lost a child ever inquired about coming, she would provide a scholarship, and our church family graciously covered everything else.

Eight months after Jensyn passed away, Chris and I flew to Marble, Colorado, to join three other pastors and their wives for a ten-day session of intensive counseling. We assumed we would spend time grieving our daughter and discussing church dynamics, and we did . . . briefly. What shocked us both was that most of our counseling time focused on us individually and as a couple. It was soon clear that we had a lot of work to do to heal our hearts and restore our relationship.

The most difficult question I get asked since losing Jensyn is, "How are you doing?" I never have a good answer—partly because I do not know how I am doing most days and because other days, I truly am doing okay, yet that feels wrong to say too. I can go from joy to sorrow and back again in just moments. But anytime someone asks me how my marriage is, I have always said it is great. Chris was a rock through everything. Of course, I could see the stress, the pain, the loss, the grief—all the feelings we were both experiencing—but I never doubted our connection with each other. Yet, in Colorado, our counselor began our first couple's session with that very question:

"How are you doing?" she asked.

"We're good," we answered.

"I don't believe you," she challenged.

This began an in-depth, intense exploration of our marriage and recognizing the reality of our relationship as it was then—eight months after losing our daughter, years after living in survival mode. What was unveiled for us was a very different image than what we had convinced ourselves was accurate—and now there was more to grieve.

After miscarrying our first child, I remember telling Chris that even though losing our baby was extremely hard, as long as I had him, we could get through anything. Over time, that belief remained strong, yet because of Britlyn's and Jensyn's many needs, life chipped away at our connection. Like any erosion, it was a slow fade, a little bit at a time. And in the midst of our crazy, it went unnoticed and, ultimately, unaddressed. We just did the next thing, made the next decision, pushed forward, and pressed on. It took someone else to uncover and lay bare our current condition: in the process of providing for our family, we did not prioritize each other.

Our commitment to "oneness" creates the bond that holds us together, and we have absolutely been a team in meeting our family's needs, but serving others became our focus, which, in turn, made our relationship fuzzy. Yet, in God's goodness, He provided a way for us to recognize this fracture, these unknown fragments of ourselves, and define them. As with anything, once something is exposed, it can be restored. So, we have been tasked with some tangible ways of making time for each other and being intentional as we work to rebuild on the foundation that was established almost thirty years ago. We have implemented weekly "Check-in Chats" to ensure we are on the same page, and we are doing what we can to create space for each other through date nights and uninterrupted time together. I am so grateful for my husband, who, in humility, continues to fight for his family and for me.

From the moment Jensyn was born, she showed our family how to fight for what is important, and what God has taught us through her short life is priceless. A few days after she passed away, we received a letter that wrecked us. It painted a picture we never thought to paint. It gave us a glimpse of God and of his intentional purpose for our girl. Another friend who had never met Jensyn shared something God revealed to her cousin during a time of prayer they had for Jensyn two days before she died:

I was praying for Jensyn and asked God about her life and the physical struggles she had to endure. He

said that before she came to earth, she agreed to this
mission to be a witness, particularly to the medical
community, through her and through her family. She
knew the physical suffering she would endure, and she
accepted the assignment. When her spirit cries out to
Me that she is tired and ready to come home, I will
take her home.

We will never know this side of heaven if this word about Jensyn is true, if Jensyn really knew about an assignment from God, but we saw God use her as a witness of His goodness over and over again. And, I can hardly comprehend that God allowed us to be the family to serve her. Grateful does not begin to express the overwhelming feeling of that gift.

We never described Jensyn as a missionary, but it fits her so well. Jensyn had a special connection with Jesus, a hidden holiness. God gave her a sweet spirit, and there was something remarkable about her ripple effect on people, how she touched and changed lives. Jensyn became our common denominator, our example of pure, unselfish, accepting love. And somehow, in one of the greatest miracles we have witnessed in this life, she made us better people and, ultimately, a stronger family.

And she did it without speaking a word.

EPILOGUE:
ONE LAST LETTER TO MY GIRL

My Sweet Jensy Marce,

I loved writing in your journals over the years, so I thought I would wrap up your story by writing to you one last time, to update you on how difficult it has been to learn to live without you. I always thought grief was linear—that we would go from stage to stage—but I am learning it is anything but. Feelings and emotions and numbness exist all at the same time, and the lines get blurred and jumbled. I wonder if things will ever straighten out again.

Yet, in the grief, we have seen God's goodness. We have discovered ways to honor you. This summer, a family from church blessed us with a week at their cabin. It was glaringly obvious that we were only able to be there because you were not, but it was such a special time together. Later in the summer, we took a family trip to visit Grandma Sally and Grandpa Pat in Aberdeen, South Dakota, for the first time in five years. My high school friends bought a brick at Storybook Land in your memory. Seeing your name in stone was the highlight of our trip. Even though your presence was missed immensely, these became new opportunities for us to be together and to make new memories.

We celebrated your first birthday in heaven, Jensyn. Our entire family, along with Denice, met at your gravesite. You know how much your mama loves traditions, so of course I wanted us to do something special. We wrote letters to you, Jensy! We told you how we were feeling, what has been happening since you've been gone, and what our hopes are for this next year.

We put them in a box with the plan to read them together next year, anticipating more change and growth before that time. Next September 9, we will write you new letters to read the following year. This is just a tangible way to continue doing life with you, sweet girl. Of course, we know this has more to do with our own healing than anything else.

Unfortunately, you did not get to meet Maci and Chase's son, the one they told us about when you were in the hospital during Thanksgiving of 2022, but the rest of us celebrated when Judah Jensyn was born in July. Maci shared at your funeral that the last thing she told you was the name they had chosen for their son. We could always trust you to keep our secrets! You have a niece named after you as well. Max and Sidney had Haven Marcella in October. You know that I think names are a big deal, but your siblings believe you are a bigger deal. What a gift it is to our family that God chose to bless us with two healthy, precious lives that honor your name—Jensyn Marcella. Judah and Haven are daily reminders of how much you will always mean to all of us.

One of the hardest moments, Jens, was selling Ruby. We had so many wonderful trips to appointments in that van, and for some reason, it was another place where I felt close to you. For the longest time, we had nobody interested in buying it, but God's timing always trumps ours. This past Thanksgiving, a family from South Dakota came to check it out. They have a fifteen-year-old son who is in a wheelchair, but they have never had a handicapped van. I was not home when they came to pick it up, but Dad called to tell me Ruby was gone. I immediately cried as I walked around Sam's Club. It felt like my last connection to you, yet it felt silly to be crying over a van at the same time. Grief is like that, Jensy—it hits me crazy at the strangest of times. Later that night, the boy's mom reached out to me to tell me more of their story. It meant everything to me that she would help me connect the dots. You and her son had many of the same doctors and other medical situations. I shared with her that we loved Ruby and that if she ever had any questions, she should let me know. Then she told me this:

> *"You won't believe this . . . but on the long ride home*
> *last night, I was thinking this van needed a name.*
> *When we got home, I told my husband I thought her*
> *name should be Ruby. Actually, I said it should be*
> *Ruby J. The J is for Jensyn. How amazing and not at*
> *all coincidental that you had named her that. God is*
> *so kind. He is so good to place us in the paths exactly*
> *where we need to be."*

Ruby J! It is perfect. Even in your death, you are still connecting lives, Jensyn! God continues to show us His goodness.

As things have continued to unravel and we have been able to define the broken pieces of our hearts, it has become clear that talking about you offers the first step toward the feeling needed for healing. Many of your siblings have started individual counseling. Dad and I continue to work through what was revealed at our counseling intensive in Colorado, and the rest of the family hopes to begin meeting with professionals who can help them process things as well. Grief affects so many different areas of life, and it truly does not look the same for everyone. For a while, it was easier to stay numb and to ignore the gigantic hole in our family—just to gut it out and move on—but we have learned that doing this only adds to the jumbled, crisscrossed mess of grieving. Eventually, we have had to press into the only One with the power to straighten out this crazy, the One who holds the ultimate plan. Slowly, together, we are beginning to move forward.

We all love to visit your gravesite, Jensyn. We know you are not there, but it brings us comfort to be there anyway. The entire family wants the space to reflect you and be a beautiful spot. Sometimes, when I visit, I just play worship music and sit with you. Worship—oh how your absence has changed this for me. I have always loved singing and worshiping, but when I picture you, happy and whole, singing to the Lord in heaven, I am wrecked. It has transformed everything about the way I approach my own worship and makes me excited for you in yours. I cannot wait to physically worship with you someday.

And then it was your first Heaven Day! The days leading up to the anniversary of your passing were weirdly more brutal than the actual day in some ways. Anticipatory grief, I guess it is called. As we remembered our final week with you, we were each affected differently. March 10 was a Sunday this year. Ironically, Tate had a soccer game during church. Skipping church for a sport has never been our thing, but we needed to be together.

Tate's team heard that this day was going to be difficult for our family, so to honor you on behalf of Tate, they wore "4 Jensyn" written on green tape around their wrists, our goalie sported his green uniform, and when one of Tate's teammates received the opportunity to take a penalty kick, he humbly allowed Tate to kick it instead. For Tate to score a goal in a game dedicated to you meant everything to our family.

After the game, we joined Max, Maci, Tygen, and Sidney at the local tattoo shop. It was time to get our sloths inked. Maci, Tygen, and Max already had theirs done—each somewhat similar yet unique in their memories of you. I was next to go, with Sidney, Dad, and Chase to follow. We had been planning these permanent reminders since shortly after you passed—and to have been able to get them done on the anniversary of your Heaven Day felt like a gift. Denice joined us for part of the day and went with us to visit your grave. We finished our time together doing the last thing we did with you. Tate played piano, Max played guitar, and we joined in worship, singing the songs that remind us of you with hearts of gratitude for how we have seen God's goodness in our grief. Again, it felt divine. It is hard to believe we survived an entire year without you, but I think that through it all, we have learned that no matter what happens next, somehow, we will be okay.

Dad likes to tell people that God writes the stories we would never choose to write. In my humanity, I have wondered if, given the choice, I would choose to live this part of my story again—knowing the pain, the loss, the challenge, and the grief. My answer is yes. I would choose it over and over and over again because if we had not had you, sweet Jensyn, for six and a half years, for 2,373 days, we would not have you for eternity. The value of LIFE has always been the foundation of our family, but even more important than that, it is the focus of our faith. And you have taught us, without a doubt, that God can be trusted.

Oh, how we miss you, Jensy Marce. Thank you for being my little girl and for accepting God's mission to show us that life is worth living, worth fighting for, worth wrestling with and wondering about. Because of your quiet witness, we will keep sharing your story and pointing others to Jesus. And we will continue to do . . .

Whatever it takes.

Love,

Mom

ACKNOWLEDGMENTS

I once asked my high school literature class if they read every part of a book when they start reading or if they skip to the first chapter and begin there. What I really wanted to know is if they bothered to read the "Introduction" or the "Acknowledgments" sections. It was no surprise to learn that many of them do not. I have to wonder if anyone does. I do. I devour every word of a book, and I have always thought about what I would say if ever given the chance to write my own acknowledgments.

I liken it to a writer's Golden Globe or Academy Award speech. It's the opportunity to thank the people in our lives who made it possible for us to get where we are. It feels official and important, yet it is overwhelming at the same time because there are so many people to thank, and there is a real fear that someone will be forgotten in the process. I guess, like them, I will do my best.

Growing up, I was an athlete. I played basketball and volleyball in high school. In college, I played volleyball for four years and then coached it for many years after graduation. Something I learned about myself is that I am far better in team sports than I am in individual sports. I need a team to help me win. Writing a book is no different. And, I have been blessed with the best teammates throughout this process.

In volleyball, there are parts of the game that depended on me—the serve was all me. My position on the court and my mindset during the game all factored into my individual contribution to the team's overall success. Yet, when I had off days or when my skill level did not measure up to that of the opposition, I had teammates who picked up my slack or, at the very least, encouraged me and cheered me on to help me have a better performance. Yes, writing was initially something I had to do, but whenever I hit a roadblock, when I was unsure of how to say something, or if I forgot a crucial memory, there was a team of people who was ready and willing to help me stay in the game and keep moving forward to finish well.

Years before I even had an inkling that God was giving me a story to write, people poured encouragement, belief, and genuine excitement into my life to someday write a book. Their response when I told them I was finally going to go for it was exactly what I needed on those days when it felt overwhelming or when I questioned if I could even do it at all. Their "you've got this" or "I can't wait to read your book" fueled me to keep going. I am so grateful for each person who has prayed for me, checked on me, and "suited up" with me throughout this experience.

Typically, authors choose to wrap up their acknowledgments by thanking their family at the end—save the best for last, I guess. But, I cannot imagine starting with anyone else. My husband and my kids have been my biggest fans and cheerleaders throughout it all. Chris, your support of me and the sacrifices you have made for me to be able to realize this dream means everything. You were the one who encouraged me to take the plunge initially, to reach out to the publisher and begin writing. It was you who arranged a place for me to go on a writing retreat and told me to stay as long as I needed to. And, you have always been the one who has inspired me to tackle the unknowns of life while showing me that doing things together always works better than facing life alone. You are a phenomenal father and husband—there is nobody I would rather do this life with than you. This story is as much yours as it is mine. Thank you for trusting me to tell it.

I am also eternally grateful for my kids—Max, Maci, Tygen, Tate, Brinkley, Britlyn, and Jakely! Nobody is more excited to read this book than you are. Since you were little, you have heard me talk about this dream of mine.

Now that it is finally becoming a reality, you are pumped for me. Thank you for always being my hype squad! You also have had to make sacrifices for me to be able to write. You have put up with my late nights of writing or editing, the emotional moments in my office where something had me crying again, and stretches of time where I was away to write for hours or days—you embraced it all and supported me through it. I hope I have made you proud because I am so stinking proud of each of you. Thank you for loving Jensyn with every bit of your heart and for always seeing the eternal picture in the hardest and best days we had with her. Thank you even more for agreeing that her story must be told.

Since I was a little girl, my parents have instilled in me the confidence to face many things in life—some hard, some wonderful. Not only did they help me discover my gifts and abilities, but they also provided opportunities for me to share them with others. I was encouraged to try new things without the fear of them ever being disappointed. Mom and Dad, your belief in me has allowed me to experience difficult things, knowing you have always had my back. Obviously, your support of me in writing this book has been no different. I am also grateful for the many times you came to stay with the kids when we needed to be at the hospital with Jensyn— sometimes weeks at a time—knowing that you were at home with the kids allowed us to focus on what Jensyn needed. I love you both so much.

As far as in-laws go, I have been blessed. Lowell and Linda, your commitment to cleaning our house, cooking meals, and caring for our kids when Chris and I needed to be with Jensyn at the hospital meant everything to us. You truly were with us until the very end. I am so grateful for you both.

I often tell people that I have the BEST friends. And I do. Truly, it is a gift to have lifetime friends, friends who show up when life is less than perfect, friends who roll up their sleeves and push me out of the way to serve during hard times, friends who check in with me and check up on me, friends who say they will pray and actually do. I have those friends, and I am grateful for the chance to be able to thank them for being the best. Thank you to the Homeschool Hotties—you know who you are—my BEFC prayer team, my college roommates, and my other sisters (and brothers) in Christ who have been with me through it all. I am beyond blessed by all of you.

While I am giving a shout-out to my amazing friends, I cannot forget Gretchyn Quernemoen. Thank you, Gretchyn, for being a tangible example of love and support and for obeying God when He prompted you to voice message me every morning at 9:00 a.m. after Jensyn passed away. You remembered that 9:00 was when I had my first connection with Jensyn every morning—the time for her first round of meds and treatments—and you knew that time of day would feel painfully difficult in my loss. It has meant so much to me that you would take the time to reach out each day and that you are still doing it now. Along with that, you offered to read and edit my book. I am so grateful for your insight, your encouragement, and your expertise. Your friendship is priceless. I also want to thank you and Barry for opening up part of your home to let me have several uninterrupted writing days. "The Bunker" will forever be a special place for me when I recall my writing journey. I definitely owe you a few Diet Cokes and several boxes of Kleenex!

Another place that has become dear to me throughout this process is the Wynia's cabin. Thank you, Steve and Charina—not only for gifting our entire family with a week at your cabin for our first family vacation in five years but also for allowing me to be there for almost a week to have a peaceful, reflective writing retreat. It was during my time there that God helped me write some of the most difficult chapters and where He met me late one night to finally give me my title. I will treasure this time at your place. So grateful for your generosity.

Thank you, Marcia Ericson and Tanya Grosz, for prayerfully and consistently texting me every Wednesday morning once you heard it was my designated writing day. Knowing that you were checking in held me accountable and kept me motivated to keep writing. Wednesdays spent in my office—which used to be Jensyn's bedroom—became my favorite day of the week. Jensyn and I spent every Wednesday night together when she was alive because the rest of the family was at youth group, so it was only fitting that she and I would continue to "spend" Wednesdays together as I told her story. So many prayed during this exact time each week, and I felt every prayer.

Speaking of prayer, I want to thank Denice Frieh. You were more than Jensyn's nurse; you became a friend and a mentor to me. You have consistently reached out during the months since Jensyn passed. Your check-ins to see how I am doing with grief, with writing, or even with being a mom and a wife have meant so much to me. Your continued commitment to our family is a gift, and I know you are another one who does more than just offer to pray—you intentionally do it.

I am also grateful for my mom's prayer pals—she has a huge team of faithful and devoted prayer warriors who are committed to praying as needs are made known. Their faithful investment over the years has made such a difference in our lives, and they have been just as gracious to pray for the completion of this book. Our entire journey has been covered in their prayers, and we feel so blessed.

I began this section by sharing about my volleyball career both as an athlete and a coach. By my third season in college, I had had three different coaches. But I had never had a coach like Jill Peterson. Not only did she believe in me as an athlete, but she also asked me to become her assistant coach upon my graduation. She mentored me on so many levels. The crazy thing is that we did not only have volleyball in common. We share a degree in English education, and over the years, she has helped me in that area as well. So, when she offered to read through my manuscript to edit, enhance, and comment, I was all in! Thank you, Jill. I love that you are "old school" and that you actually printed out the entire book and marked it up with your colorfully penned comments. I love to edit that way as well. Your feedback, your coaching, and your friendship in my life have meant everything, and I am so grateful that we got to be on the same team once again.

When we first received Jensyn's diagnosis, we were told that there were only fifty known cases of Trisomy 5p. Much like Britlyn's story, we took to social media to see if we could find any of these other Trisomy 5 families. The connections I made with Lorri, Hope, Ashley, and Daisy became invaluable as we walked through the uncertainties and ambiguities of our similar journeys. Unfortunately, three of Jensyn's friends—Ava, Jack, and Viggo—passed away shortly before Jensyn did. Ava and Jack were much older than Jensyn, but Viggo was just a baby. Although it was difficult for each of us to go through losing our children so close together, I am grateful that Trisomy 5 will forever connect our hearts.

After Jensyn passed away, our kids began to plot tattoos. I begrudgingly got a tattoo when Maci turned 18. Her "dream" since she was 16 was for the two of us to get tattoos when she was finally old enough. I was not interested. But, then I had a nightmare of my own. I wondered about her being so far away in Mexico and the regret I would have if something happened to her while she was there. So, I caved. We have tattoos of words written in each other's handwriting. Since then, Maci has gotten many more tattoos, and Max has one as well. I said I would never permanently mark my skin again unless something happened to Jensyn. So, when Jensyn passed, Maci, our tattoo aficionado, reached out to a friend to have her design the images she had in mind. Maci envisioned a sloth with a cannula. Her friend, Abby Colwell, brought that vision to reality. She created three different designs—one a more masculine-looking tattoo with a sloth climbing a vine, another with a sweet sloth surrounded by sunflowers, and the third was just a cute little cannula-ed sloth chilling with a gentle smile on its face. When it was time to decide on the cover of this book, I had no idea where to begin. How could I make it iconic enough to encapsulate how we see our girl? It became clear that it was not something I could create or imagine because it had already been created. Thank you, Abby, for bringing Maci's vision to life, for working with me as we tweaked and edited, and ultimately, for making the sweetest sloth icon for our family—it literally brings me joy every time I see it. The creativity of your art oozes Jensyn's personality and gentle nature. What a gift you have! Thank you for sharing it with us.

Jon Norberg! Your creativity is next-level, and I am so grateful for you and for your design input! Thank you for taking the time to look things over (and over) and share your expertise. Priceless.

I would be remiss if I didn't officially thank Casey Van Winkle, that guy from one of our first youth groups that I mentioned in my book introduction, for connecting me with my publisher, Lindsay Bednar. Casey, you and your parents have often suggested I should write a book and have always been so supportive of my writing. You took the chance to suggest this new creative endeavor with your friend from college, for which I will be forever grateful. I love that God never wastes a relationship and that our small world has remained connected.

Lindsay, my publisher—I was freaked out when I reached out to you, and I was a hot mess the first time we officially met. My grief was fresh, but you were gracious and open to hearing my heart, and you valued my story. You are so good at what you do—professional yet personable. This has meant everything as you have guided me through the process to realize this desire of my heart. I am grateful God chose to bring our lives together through this process. Thank you!

I do not know how I can ever fully express my gratitude to God for giving me the ability to write. Every good and perfect gift truly is from above, and I continue to witness His goodness every day. Never did I think this would be the story God had for me, but then again, no other story would have been more rewarding. It was a privilege to care for Jensyn, and it has been an honor to write about her life. Lord, you gave me the words, as precious as they are, and I can only hope that I stewarded them well. Thank you for allowing me to be the one to give Jensyn a voice.

ABOUT THE AUTHOR

Born and raised in Aberdeen, South Dakota, KRISTIN SALVEVOLD moved to Minnesota to attend college, where she met her husband, Chris. They currently reside in Becker, Minnesota, where Chris is a youth pastor, and she is a stay-at-home, homeschooling mom. Those who call her Mom are Max, Maci, Tygen, Tate, Brinkley, Britlyn, Jakely, and Jensyn. She is mother-in-law to Sidney and Chase, and her newest and most favorite role is that of being grandma to Crosby, Sadie, Haven, and Judah.

A self-professed word nerd, Kristin has a degree in English education and leads the local homeschool co-op, where she gets to stretch her education muscles with middle and high school students by teaching writing, literature, and speech. She is passionate about home education in all capacities and has graduated three of her children, with four more still at home.

Kristin has also been a special-needs mom to two of her daughters, which was the impetus for realizing her dream of writing a book. Her daughter, Britlyn, paved the way with therapies and delays, but when Jensyn was born, it was clear that her needs were beyond special, being more medically fragile in nature. As the family navigated life with two girls who required a bit more, their faith was strengthened as they developed indescribable bonds.

When Jensyn lost her battle with Trisomy 5p, Kristin knew it was time to share her story. Snippets of Jensyn's journey were shared for the six and a half years of her life, but the goal has always been to remain an open book—one that exposes the value of life, that expresses the capacity to care for those the world sees differently, and ultimately, that extols the One whose goodness sustains when life does not make sense.

Made in the USA
Monee, IL
02 April 2024

56252822R00195